BOUNDARY STONES

By Aaron Eby

FIRST FRUITS OF
ZION

First Fruits of Zion is a 501(c)(3) registered nonprofit educational organization.

First Edition 2008
Printed in the United States of America

ISBN: 1–892124–31–9

Cover Design: Avner Wolff

Quantity discounts are available on bulk purchases of this book for educational, fundraising, or event purposes. Special versions or book excerpts to fit specific needs are available from First Fruits of Zion. For more information, contact www.ffoz.org/contact.

First Fruits of Zion

PO Box 649, Marshfield, Missouri 65706–0649 USA
Phone (417) 468–2741, www.ffoz.org

Comments and questions: www.ffoz.org/contact

Contents

Foreword

- For the law of the Spirit of life has set you free in Christ Jesus from the law … (Romans 8:2)
- … since you are not under law but under grace. (Romans 6:14)

These snippets from Scripture are important tenets in Christianity. But what do they really mean? What, exactly, is the Law from which we have been set free? This book asks such questions about the Law and its relationship to Christians, and then attempts to offer thoughtful answers.

It is important that the reader understands the author's perspective on the Law from the outset. The "Law" is a biblical term for the first five books of the Bible: Genesis, Exodus, Leviticus, Numbers, and Deuteronomy. They are also called the "Books of Moses" because Moses wrote them. In the Hebrew language (the language in which the Old Testament was written), the first five books are collectively called the *Torah*. *Torah* is a word that means "instruction." God's intention for giving the Torah is to instruct his people in holiness:

> The LORD said to Moses, "Come up to me on the mountain and wait there, that I may give you the tablets of stone, with *the law* and the commandment, which I have written *for their instruction*." (Exodus 24:12, emphasis added)

The Torah contains the record of creation, the story of the fall of man, the plight of humanity, the call of Abraham, the exodus from Egypt, the stories of the wilderness wanderings, the covenants with Israel, and a lot of rules and instructions from God. These rules and instructions include well-known passages like the Ten Commandments and the Golden Rule: "You shall love your neighbor as yourself" (Leviticus 19:18).[1] They also include ritual laws about sacrifices, holy days, dietary restrictions, and various ceremonies. For all of the 1,400 years from the days of Moses to the days of Jesus, the Torah was the rule of life and standard of godliness for God's chosen people, Israel.

An example of a rule from the Torah (the one upon which this book is based) is the prohibition on moving a boundary stone:

> You shall not move your neighbor's landmark, which the men of old have set, in the inheritance that you will hold in the land that the LORD your God is giving you to possess. (Deuteronomy 19:14)

In biblical times, territorial borders were marked off with boundary stones. A boundary-stone landmark was one stone set on its end to indicate the border between a man's field and his neighbor's.

During the settlement of American territories, a similar method was used. Settlers set up rocks or drove stakes into the ground to indicate which parcels of land they were claiming. Hence the idiom "staking a claim" was born. Sometimes, in the claimant's absence, unscrupulous neighbors or other settlers would remove these landmarks to their own advantage. If a settler found a particularly nice piece of land, but then discovered someone else's boundary marks on it, he might move the marker over by several acres or simply dispose of it and pretend that he never saw it. He could then claim the property for himself.

Anytime an unscrupulous neighbor moved a boundary stone to claim part of his neighbor's field, it was a form of theft, prohibited by the commandment of not moving a neighbor's landmark. The Bible goes so far as to place a curse on anyone who moves a boundary stone: "'Cursed be anyone who moves his neighbor's landmark.' And all the people shall say, 'Amen'" (Deuteronomy 27:17).

The prohibition on moving a boundary stone can also be applied to the realm of theology and faith. There are boundary stones in the Christian religion that should not be moved. For example, the fundamentals of monotheism, God's unchanging character, his attributes of justice and mercy, the truth and eternal bond of his Word, etc., are all boundary stones that should not be moved.

Think of it this way: Suppose you are playing checkers with someone when they suddenly move their pieces on the wrong-colored checker squares. You say, "You can't do that; it's cheating. That's not in the rules." The person replies, "I have changed the rules." If this happens, your friend is no longer playing checkers; he is playing some other game that he made up.

This is a book about biblical boundary stones. The essentials of the Bible are true and must remain effectual if our religion is real. These theological boundary markers are like the rules of the checkers game. If we are not playing by the rules, we are playing some other game, but it's not biblical Christianity.

This book is not, however, a treatise of creed-like affirmations or a comprehensive list of Christian fundamentals. Instead, it is an inquiry into Christianity's relationship with the law of Moses. It is an examination of several important, theological landmarks about the Law that stake out the territory of biblical faith. If any of these landmarks are moved or removed, the integrity of the Bible will be compromised.

Apprehending biblical faith requires that each one of us takes responsibility to study the Scriptures, ask questions, seek answers, learn, and grow. This does not negate the authority of one's clergy or denominational tradition, but it is healthy to take a personal interest in one's own belief, rather than just taking someone else's word for it.

That said, you should know something about the author of this book and the ministry that is publishing it. Aaron Eby is a writer and translator for the ministry of First Fruits of Zion, a Messianic Jewish publishing and educational ministry that teaches about early Christianity and its intersection with Judaism. The ministry of First Fruits of Zion espouses a path of discipleship to Jesus of Nazareth that includes the practice of what some Christians might commonly call "Old Testament Law." We encourage all believers to take hold of their full biblical heritage—including the Torah of Moses—not for the sake of earning righteousness, but for the sake of discipleship to Jesus. The goal of our ministry is not to make Christians Jewish, but to help Christians be good disciples of our Jewish Messiah.

Aaron Eby is of Jewish descent, is raising a Jewish family, and is a disciple of Jesus. He lives with his wife and four young children in Hudson, Wisconsin, where he attends a Messianic congregation. He grew up in a Pentecostal church but now expresses his faith in Jesus through the practice of a traditional Jewish lifestyle. He is a teacher of biblical Hebrew, the principal translator of several prayer resources, and the author of several books and articles for First Fruits of Zion. Among those contributions is a series of articles titled "Boundary Stones," originally published in First Fruits of Zion's periodical *messiah magazine*. The chapters of this book are a collection of Eby's articles.

This may be difficult material, but not in the sense of being hard to understand. The logic is actually very simple. Yet it is rather difficult in the sense that it challenges long-held assumptions; it forces us to rethink our Christian paradigms.

The premise of each chapter is that the Torah of God is an enduring and central part of the Bible, not done away with or cancelled by the New Testament. Rather than something from which Christians have been set free, the Torah can be viewed as

God's loving instruction to his people and the revelation of his will and wisdom. The Torah has something to say to all believers—even today.

This book is not meant to de-legitimize Christianity or to make the reader feel insecure about his or her relationship with God. There is no condemnation here, only an earnest entreaty to think through some things together. I invite the reader to consider the theological boundary stones presented in this book and then come to his or her own conclusions. Even if you do not agree with the contents of the book, you will be challenged to decide exactly where the original boundary stones are supposed to be. And that's a good thing.

Boaz Michael

FOUNDER AND DIRECTOR,
FIRST FRUITS OF ZION

Salvation Is by Grace

Key Points

- People received forgiveness by faith in the Messiah even before he came.
- These people faithfully and lovingly continued to observe God's revealed Law.
- The Law did not serve as a means of gaining salvation prior to the Messiah but as an eternal guide to a life of faith.

Grace Alone

It is clear from Scripture that we have all erred. We have all made mistakes in our lives and have fallen short of God's perfect plan. Romans 3:23 solidifies this point: "All have sinned and fall short of the glory of God." As a result, the penalty for sin is death: "For the wages of sin is death, but the free gift of God is eternal life in Christ Jesus our Lord" (Romans 6:23). As a righteous judge, God finds us guilty and is just in condemning us. Our own wrongdoings have separated us from God.

But in his mercy, God extends forgiveness to us, as the second half of Romans 6:23 points out. Through his death and resurrection, Jesus, the Son of God, paid the penalty that we deserved. When we put our trust in him and turn from our lives of sin, Jesus' own righteousness is applied to us: "For our sake he made him to be sin who knew no sin, so that in him we might become the righteousness of God" (2 Corinthians 5:21).

Tough Question

So, let's now ask a tough question: What about people who died before Jesus came? Have they all gone to hell because their sins had not yet been paid for on the cross?

Think about the great heroes of the past: Abraham, Isaac, Jacob, Moses, David, and Elijah. All of these men seemed to be in some kind of relationship with God, yet even these great men were not faultless. They sinned just as we have. Numerous times we read of them lying, committing murder, or disobeying God. According to God's own standard, they deserve to be punished.

However, we know that Abraham, Isaac, and Jacob are receiving their eternal reward. Our master and teacher, Jesus, states, "I tell you, many will come from east and west and recline at table with Abraham, Isaac, and Jacob in the kingdom of heaven" (Matthew 8:11).

We also know that Moses talked to God face to face according to Numbers 12:8, and he and Elijah appeared to Peter, James, and John at the transfiguration (Matthew 17:3; et al.). Even though David committed some very grievous sins, he was still called a man after God's own heart (1 Samuel 13:14 and Acts 13:22). It seems reasonable, then, to assume that both of these men will be in heavenly paradise. Furthermore, it is written that Elijah actually ascended to heaven in a chariot (2 Kings 2:11).

None of these great men fully obeyed every written commandment, yet in some way they must have been forgiven of their faults—even before Jesus' sacrifice.

Many people believe that those who lived before Jesus gained forgiveness from their sins through offering animal sacrifices. This is a common belief, especially in light of verses like Leviticus 17:11, which says, "For it is the blood that makes atonement by the life." However, the writer of Hebrews makes it absolutely clear that "it is impossible for the blood of bulls and goats to take away sins" (Hebrews 10:4). Offering sacrifices cannot perfect the worshiper (Hebrews 9:9, 10:1). That's not what the sacrificial system was designed to do.

If animal sacrifices and/or obedience to the commandments of God could bring eternal forgiveness to our souls, then Jesus wouldn't have had to die for our sins. There would have been no need for God to send his precious Son to be tortured to death! Galatians 2:21 states, "I do not nullify the grace of God, for if righteousness were through the law, then Christ died for no purpose."

The heroes of faith did not keep every single commandment perfectly, nor were they able to remove their sins through offering sacrifices.

Faith

Romans chapter 4 explains that God's grace comes by faith alone and cannot be earned. Paul supports this claim by quoting from Genesis 15:6, which says that Abraham "believed the LORD, and [God] counted it to [Abraham] as righteousness."

Abraham received righteousness by grace through faith, which is—and always has been—the only way for anyone to receive right standing before God and forgiveness for sin. Any other heroes whom we will see in Paradise will undoubtedly have obtained righteousness in this fashion.

In fact, the faith of these devout ones is attested to in Hebrews 11, demonstrating that their faith led to their eternal reward: "But as it is, they desire a better country, that is, a heavenly one. Therefore God is not ashamed to be called their God, for he has prepared for them a city" (Hebrews 11:16).

But wait. At this point in history Jesus hadn't died for the world's sins, had he? Jesus himself said, "I am the way, and the truth, and the life. No one comes to the Father except through

They began to obey the Law in faith because it is God's revealed will.

me" (John 14:6). Is it possible that Abraham came to the Father through some other means? Absolutely not! If he had, then the words of our own Messiah would be a lie, and he is not a liar. Thus Abraham must have been made righteous and reconciled to God through Jesus.

In Temple times, people didn't offer a sacrifice before sinning; they offered it after they sinned. Sacrifices applied retroactively. In the same way, Jesus' sacrifice did not apply only to the future, but, in a timeless way, it was the means by which the Lord granted grace to those in the past. Hebrews 4:3 affirms the timelessness of Messiah's sacrifice: "His works were finished from the foundation of the world."

Genesis 15:6 says that Abraham "believed the LORD." He believed in the promises of redemption and blessing; he looked forward in time with belief, and he longed for that time of the coming Messiah. Paul even proclaims that the gospel was preached to Abraham beforehand. (See Galatians 3:8.)

Moreover, Jesus said Abraham "rejoiced that he would see my day. He saw it and was glad" (John 8:56). Since God's Spirit showed this vision of redemption to Abraham, we can assume he did likewise to others.

Every person since Adam only comes to the Father by grace through faith. This faith is through God's promised Redeemer. God sent the Redeemer and will send him again at the end of days. Now we, like the ancient heroes, await his coming through an act of faith.

Now What?

In some ways, addressing how pre-Jesus saints were saved raises more questions than it answers. For example, if Moses received grace through faith, why did he also receive the Law on Mount Sinai? If grace was already around in Abraham's day, why did God dole out all the commandments hundreds of years later? If Paul was correct in saying that King David understood forgiveness by grace (Romans 4:5–8), why does David write the longest chapter in the Bible (Psalm 119) as an ode to God's Law?

Perhaps we have misunderstood the reason for the Law. This author proposes that it was not given to help people become perfect. Its purpose was never to enable people to merit eternal salvation. The ancient people of Israel did not obey the commandments in order to earn right standing before God. Like religious Jews today, they knew that they could not keep every detail perfectly, so they turned to God in repentance and trusted in him for forgiveness.

They began to obey the Law in faith because it is God's revealed will. They did so because they loved God and because it is what he asked of them. As 1 John 5:3 states, "For this is the love of God, that we keep his commandments. And his commandments are not burdensome." They also knew that God knows more than we do (Isaiah 55:8–9) and that he has our best interest in mind. A lifestyle founded on the holy, good, and righteous Law of God (Romans 7:12) is the natural result of a heart of faith.

You may already know that the Law shows us our need for a savior. It condemns us of our sin. It leads us to find and accept the Messiah. All of these things are absolutely true, and they apply to those who have not yet come to faith in God through the Messiah.

But after we come to faith in Jesus, we have a new relationship to the Law. Now that our sins—our failures to keep the Law—have been taken away (1 John 3:5), we can begin to carry out God's instructions, simply because we love him and it is what he has asked us to do.

A Life of Faith

We know that everyone has sinned (disobeyed God's Law) and deserves death. We also know that God grants forgiveness through his Son, who paid our penalty.

Even the great heroes of faith committed sin, yet they will be with us in our eternal reward. Their sins needed forgiveness, just as ours do today. Neither observance of commandments nor sacrifices could save them. It was only through faith in the future redemption and the promise of the Messiah that God granted them grace and forgiveness.

As we await the fulfillment of the promise of the Messiah's return, we can learn from the "great cloud of witnesses" (Hebrews 12:1) that has gone before us. They lived out lives of faith, putting their love for God into practice as they followed the commandments in his holy Law.

Salvation Is by Grace

Through him we have also obtained access by faith into this grace in which we stand. (Romans 5:2)

Keeping the Law in order to merit or maintain salvation is outside of the boundaries of biblical faith. Even before Messiah came, people received forgiveness for sin and the gift of grace through faith. Heroes of the Bible like Abraham, Moses, Joshua, and David were saved by grace, not by keeping the Law. God did not give his people the Law as a way for them to earn salvation. Instead, the Law was meant to be a guide for the life of faith. People kept the Law because they were faithful to God; they loved him and desired to obey his commandments.

Sin Is Defined by the Law

Key Points

- *Sin* is defined by Scripture as breaking the commandments of the Law.
- Our forgiveness and freedom in the Messiah do not grant us license to sin.
- Those who have received God's forgiveness would do well to seek to carry out his will as expressed in the Law.

Right and Wrong

All have sinned and fall short of God's glory.[2] The wages of sin is death.[3] Jesus came to save us from our sins.[4] We're sinners saved by grace.[5]

Sin is a church word. Hardly anybody ever says it outside of a faith context. However, even within a faith context, people understand this term to mean many different things. So let's take a moment to define *sin* according to what Scripture says.

The main word for sin in the Bible is the Hebrew word *chet*. It comes from a word root meaning "to miss the mark." It invokes imagery of an archer taking aim and firing an arrow, only to miss his intended target. Sin is clearly some kind of wrongdoing: an error, a fault, or a mistake.

It stands to reason that if sin is doing the wrong thing, there must be a right thing. In order for an archer to miss, he must be aiming for something.

If sin is so serious that it condemns us to death, there must be some way to know if something we are doing is wrong (a sin) or right (not a sin). There must be a clear definition for the standard of righteousness. When a man stands before the righteous Judge and is condemned as guilty because of his sins, there must be something definitive by which to condemn him.

The Biblical Definition

The Bible provides the definition for sin. 1 John 3:4 states, "Everyone who makes a practice of sinning also practices lawlessness; sin is lawlessness." The Greek word for lawlessness is *anomia*, from the prefix *a-* meaning "without," and *nomos*, meaning "law." The Hebrew term corresponding to *nomos* is *torah*.[6]

The Greek *nomos*, and the Hebrew *torah*, most often refer to the books of the Law, which were written by Moses: Genesis, Exodus, Leviticus, Numbers, and Deuteronomy.[7] These books contain teachings, stories, and commandments, including the commandments given on Mount Sinai.

The Ten Commandments, for example, are included in the Law or Torah. Some commandments in the Torah prohibit acts such as stealing, murder, and certain sexual unions. Others speak to civil disputes, such as inheritance or the destruction of property. We also find laws that prohibit eating certain animals as well as participating in self-mutilation or idolatrous practices. The Torah instructs about holy days of the year and the observance of the weekly Sabbath. Also, some commandments are targeted only to the Israelite priesthood, instructing them about sacrifices and worship within the Tabernacle.

Even prior to God giving the Law at Mount Sinai, the Law still existed in a rudimentary form; however, it had not been revealed on a national level. For example, God said of Abraham that he "obeyed my voice and kept my charge, my commandments, my statutes, and my laws" (Genesis 26:5).

As John writes, sin is *anomia*: disobedience to God's Law. That means that when God condemns a person because of his sins, that person is being judged guilty of breaking the commandments found in the Law of God.

Paul makes the statement that "the law brings wrath, but where there is no law there is no transgression" (Romans 4:15). In other words, if there were no commandments to break, then no one would be guilty. But because God gave commandments in the Law, it is possible to sin, and therefore God's punishment is justified. Remember the archer? He cannot miss unless there is a target for which he is aiming. One who claims to be a skilled archer can turn out to be quite poor when a target is presented to him.

Paul also says, "The sting of death is sin, and the power of sin is the law" (1 Corinthians 15:56). We are condemned to death because of our sins, and our sins are judged according to the Law. Romans 7:7 confirms this interpretation:

> What then shall we say? That the law is sin? By no means! Yet if it had not been for the law, I would not have known sin. For I would not have known what it is to covet if the law had not said, "You shall not covet."

Similarly, when a man is convicted of a crime by an earthly judge, it is the laws of the land that give power to the prosecutor to accuse him, to the jury to convict him, and to the judge to sentence him. That certainly does not mean that such laws are bad. On the contrary, they are good and necessary for a healthy society. Similarly, Paul writes, "So the law is holy, and the commandment is holy and righteous and good" (Romans 7:12).

Thus Scripture defines sin as any failure to obey the commandments in God's Law.

If sin is so serious that it condemns us to death, there must be some way to know if something we are doing is wrong (a sin) or right (not a sin).

Forgiveness and Freedom

It's a good thing the story doesn't end there, because we all fail to obey God's commandments fully. Only the Messiah Jesus himself fully obeyed every applicable commandment found in the Law.[8] In his death he paid the penalty for breaking the Law that was due us, and by faith in him we receive the gift of eternal life. Thank God that our eternal status does not depend on our ability to perform all the commandments.

Before we received his payment, our sinful lives were compared to the Law, and the Law's prescribed punishment—death—applied to us. But now, the Law's punishment does not apply to us, due to the grace of God. Now we've found freedom. We were once in bondage, but now we are free!

Yet the freedom we receive in Messiah is not freedom from God's Law. It is freedom from the law of sin and death.[9] Because we are free from sin (now able to resist its temptation by the power of God's Spirit within us), we are also free from the penalty of sin that is found in the Law: death.

We should not feel free to commit sins, now that by God's grace they are forgiven. As it is written, "What then? Are we to sin because we are not under law but under grace? By no means!" (Romans 6:15).

In fact, now that we are new creations, we are finally able to begin obeying God's commandments as an affirmation of our love for him. That's why Paul wrote,

> Let not sin therefore reign in your mortal body, to make you obey its passions. Do not present your

members to sin as instruments for unrighteousness, but present yourselves to God as those who have been brought from death to life, and your members to God as instruments for righteousness. For sin will have no dominion over you, since you are not under law but under grace. (Romans 6:12–14)

In Jesus, we are free from our bondage to sin. Sin is breaking God's commandments. Now we are able to serve God as instruments of righteousness and to obey his commandments.

In fact, if we continue to lead a life of sin, it would appear that we are still in bondage. If we remain in bondage to sin, then we must not be new creations. If we are not new creations, then we most certainly have not received God's gift of grace by faith. If we are obedient to sin, then by definition we are slaves to sin. If we are obedient to God's commandments, then we are slaves to God. As Paul states,

Do you not know that if you present yourselves to anyone as obedient slaves, you are slaves of the one whom you obey, either of sin, which leads to death, or of obedience, which leads to righteousness? (Romans 6:16)

Jesus did not come only to forgive our sins but to completely take them away. If they are taken away, then why should they remain with us? The Apostle John states,

You know that he appeared to take away sins, and in him there is no sin. No one who abides in him keeps on sinning; no one who keeps on sinning has either seen him or known him. (1 John 3:5–6)

Taking Aim

As we have learned, the Hebrew word for the Law is Torah. Torah literally means "teaching, guidance, or instruction." The word

Torah comes from the root verb *yarah*, which means "to shoot an arrow."

Sin is missing the mark; sin is falling short of God's righteous standard. God's righteous standard is the commandments of the Law. Scripture defines sin as any failure to obey those commandments. The penalty for breaking the commandments is death. But the penalty has been paid for those who have faith in Jesus.

Through God's gift of grace in Jesus, we now have a new relationship to the Law. Before, it condemned us, but now it teaches us how we can serve God as instruments of righteousness.

Sin Is Defined by the Law

Everyone who makes a practice of sinning also practices lawlessness; sin is lawlessness. (1 John 3:4)

In the Bible, the word *sin* refers to breaking one of the commandments. Though every human being is guilty of sinning against God by breaking his Law, believers receive forgiveness for their sins by faith in Messiah. The Messiah sets us free from sin. However, to be clear: Being "set free from sin" is not the same as being "free to sin." Being saved makes it unacceptable for us to continue habitually living in sin. A person who has been forgiven and set free from sin will try to avoid sinning further. Avoiding sin requires keeping God's Law.

God's People Are His Servants

Key Points

- Before our redemption, we were enslaved to sin and unable to obey God's Law.
- When God redeemed us, he took us out of our bondage to sin.
- Through spiritual rebirth, we are granted the ability to lead lives of righteousness.

Slavery and Freedom

Scripture frequently frames salvation in terms of slavery and freedom. This salvation, "by the washing of regeneration and renewing by the Holy Spirit" (Titus 3:5), is not just an end but also a new beginning. Our new identity is in the Messiah, and now we can seek to live righteous and godly lives according to God's revealed will. Since the burden of sin is removed from us, we desire to serve God and keep his commandments.

Slaves to Sin

In an unredeemed state, we stand utterly condemned. Try as we may, we cannot earn enough merit or favor to be acceptable to God. This is because we are held in bondage to sin and controlled by our sinful inclination. In this state, it is perfectly clear that we are not able to lead lives that are pleasing to God.

The Scriptures explain that a mind that is not renewed by the Holy Spirit finds only death:

> For to set the mind on the flesh is death, but to set the mind on the Spirit is life and peace. For the mind that is set on the flesh is hostile to God, for it does not submit to God's law; indeed, it cannot. Those who are in the flesh cannot please God. (Romans 8:6–8)

This inability to submit to God's Torah carries over into the imagery of slavery and freedom:

> Do you not know that if you present yourselves to anyone as obedient slaves, you are slaves of the one whom you obey, either of sin, which leads to death, or of obedience, which leads to righteousness? But thanks be to God, that you who were once slaves of sin have become obedient from the heart to the standard of teaching to which you were committed, and, having been set free from sin, have become slaves of righteousness. I am speaking in human terms, because of your natural limitations. For just as you once presented your members as slaves to impurity and to lawlessness [*anomia*] leading to more lawlessness [*anomia*], so now present your members as slaves to righteousness leading to sanctification. (Romans 6:16–19)

At the time Paul wrote his letter to the Romans, slavery was a common institution with which the original readers would have been familiar. However, Paul's reference to freedom from slavery by God's power specifically invokes the imagery of the exodus from Egypt. Paul makes this clear when he indicates that people who are free from slavery to sin are not merely self-determining; they become slaves to a new master—to God and to righteousness. This is an allusion to the Torah, which says, "For it is to me that the people of Israel are servants. They are my servants whom I brought out of the land of Egypt: I am the LORD your God" (Leviticus 25:55).

The Hebrew term translated here as "servant" (*eved*) is the same word translated "slave" elsewhere. The imagery of the Israelite slaves in Egypt is particularly apt. Because of their burdens under Egyptian rule, it would have been impossible for them to obey the Torah's commands. They could not choose to rest on the Sabbath day. They could not be selective about their food. They had no ability to present offerings to God. While slaves in Egypt, the Israelites could not have accepted the Law of God. Thus, when God saved the Israelites from slavery in Egypt, he was finally enabling them to carry out his will.

A Transfer of Ownership

This transfer of ownership from Pharaoh to God and from sin to righteousness is what the Scripture means when it speaks of redemption. When the Bible says that God "redeemed" us, that means that he bought us back, transferring our ownership to himself. This redemption and ownership is foundational to God's authority over us.

Paul also employs this imagery in his letter to Titus:

> For the grace of God has appeared, bringing salvation for all people, training us to renounce ungodliness and worldly passions, and to live self-controlled, upright, and godly lives in the present age, waiting for our blessed hope, the appearing of the glory of our great God and Savior Jesus Christ, who gave himself for us to redeem us from all lawlessness [*anomia*] and to purify for himself a people for his own possession who are zealous for good works. (Titus 2:11–14)

Like the exodus from Egypt, a salvation from slavery has come once again—this time not merely to the Jewish people

Not only does our love for God motivate us to carry out his commandments, but we are now zealous in doing so.

but to "all people." Grace did not come to put an end to lawful observance, but to enable all people—both Jews and Gentiles—to put aside sin and unrighteousness and to carry out God's commands.

The phrase "to purify for himself a people for his own possession" is an allusion to the words of the prophets, particularly Ezekiel, who says,

> They shall not defile themselves anymore with their idols and their detestable things, or with any of their transgressions. But *I will save them* from all the backslidings in which they have sinned, and *will cleanse them; and they shall be my people*, and I will be their God. (Ezekiel 37:23, emphasis added)

Ezekiel continues by describing life under the reign of the Messiah, Son of David: "My servant David shall be king over them, and they shall all have one shepherd. They shall walk in my rules and be careful to obey my statutes" (Ezekiel 37:24).

It is common to hear believers remark that, in Jesus, they are "free from the law." However, the redemption through Jesus does not free us from the obligations of the Torah. The letter to the Romans says that we are free "from the law of sin and death" (Romans 8:2) and "set free from sin" (Romans 6:18).

The text from Titus quoted above clarifies further that Jesus came to redeem us, not from the Torah, but from "lawlessness," which is disobedience to the Torah. We were once like the ancient Israelite slaves, prevented from keeping the Torah because of our spiritual condition. But because of our redemption, we are now free from our compulsion to violate the law.

God gives us the power to submit to his Torah as a part of our spiritual regeneration through the Messiah.

Our Transformation

God transforms our very identity, allowing us to serve and please him. We are truly changed, as the Holy Spirit begins the work of purifying and sanctifying our lives. The Scripture says, "Therefore, if anyone is in Christ, he is a new creation. The old has passed away; behold, the new has come" (2 Corinthians 5:17).

We who have received forgiveness by faith in Messiah should be certain

> … to put off your old self, which belongs to your former manner of life and is corrupt through deceitful desires, and to be renewed in the spirit of your minds, and to put on the new self, created after the likeness of God in true righteousness and holiness. (Ephesians 4:22–24)

This regeneration of spirit through Messiah is not just something extra that may happen when forgiveness comes; it is an essential part of the work God does when we place our identity in Jesus. The Master himself said, "Unless one is born again, he cannot see the kingdom of God" (John 3:3). Being "born again" is not merely the recital of a certain prayer or the joining of a certain church; it is an inward and spiritual transformation.

In Romans 6, Paul describes our transformation as uniting with Messiah in his death and resurrection so that we can walk in "newness of life." Our freedom from slavery to sin is precisely what makes our lives "new." He admonishes his readers: "present your members as slaves to righteousness leading to sanctification" (Romans 6:19).

When we come to God in repentance and put faith in the Messiah, we become right with God—an event theologians commonly refer to as "justification." At that moment, we embark upon the journey of a changed life that more closely reflects God's will each day. This is the process of "sanctification."

Sanctification literally means "the act of making something holy." It is not the same as "justification." A holy thing is something that has been set apart for God. Making God's people holy by setting them apart is one important purpose of the commandments in the Torah. Peter explains: "As he who called you is holy, you also be holy in all your conduct, since it is written, 'You shall be holy, for I am holy'" (1 Peter 1:15–16, citing a passage in Leviticus 11:44, 19:2, and 20:7).

Some suggest that striving to live a godly life according to the Torah is "adding to the finished work of Messiah." This is not true. We have already received God's acceptance by faith; our motivation for obedience to his Law is love. The Scriptures themselves define "love of God" as obedience to his commandments. The Apostle John made it clear when he explained, "For this is the love of God, that we keep his commandments. And his commandments are not burdensome" (1 John 5:3). In another letter he wrote, "And this is love, that we walk according to his commandments; this is the commandment, just as you have heard from the beginning, so that you should walk in it" (2 John 1:6).

The Torah itself is the first place we learn that love for God means obedience to him. It says, "You shall therefore love the LORD your God and keep his charge, his statutes, his rules, and his commandments always" (Deuteronomy 11:1).

The letter to Titus says that Jesus gave himself "to purify for himself a people for his own possession who are zealous for good works" (Titus 2:14). Not only does our love for God motivate us to carry out his commandments, but we are now zealous in doing so. It becomes our passion.

If we live transformed lives, we will outwardly express our love for God by zealously seeking to please and obey him. If our lives do not reflect transformation, it is evidence that we did not come to God by faith. The beloved disciple tells us that the Messiah "appeared to take away sins, and in him there is no sin" (1 John 3:5). His intent is to illustrate that if Jesus took away our sins, we should not have them anymore! Since he never broke the Torah's commandments, we who are united with him should not continue in sin either. John continues with difficult but trustworthy statements:

> No one who abides in him keeps on sinning; no one who keeps on sinning has either seen him or known him. Little children, let no one deceive you. Whoever practices righteousness is righteous, as he is righteous. (1 John 3:6–7)

Ultimately, this teaches us that we are no longer just "sinners saved by grace." We were sinners once, but now we are free from sin and our identity is found in him. Now when we sin (and John readily admits that it happens[10]), we are living inconsistently with our true identity in the Messiah.

Our New Lives

Before we came to faith, we were utterly corrupt. As we read: "Those who are in the flesh cannot please God" (Romans 8:8). Thankfully, Paul did not stop there. He continues: "You, however, are not in the flesh but in the Spirit, if in fact the Spirit of God dwells in you. Anyone who does not have the Spirit of Christ does not belong to him" (Romans 8:9).

If the Spirit of God dwells in us, then we naturally aim to reflect God's righteous standard in our lives. Living a life of obedience to the Bible's commands is not adding to the work of Messiah, it is the result of the work of Messiah. It is the process of the Spirit of God setting us apart to him. It is God's handwritten recipe for a love relationship with him. It is the result of the freedom we have in the Messiah. We are new and free people; let us lead new lives!

God's People Are His Servants

But now that you have been set free from sin and have become slaves of God. (Romans 6:22)

Human beings are born sinners. Human beings are reborn as "the righteousness of God" in Messiah.[11] Before receiving salvation through faith in Jesus Christ, a person is in spiritual and legal bondage to sin, unable to keep God's Law. God redeems us through his Son, Jesus, just as he redeemed the children of Israel from slavery in Egypt. He rescues us out of our bondage to sin. Just as he set the children of Israel free from Egypt so that they could serve him, God sets us free from sin to be slaves of righteousness. He gives every believer a spiritual rebirth through which we are granted the ability to lead lives of righteousness.

Torah and Spirit Are Not Opposites

Key Points

- There is no contradiction between being led by the Spirit and being obedient to the Law.
- The Law that Jesus taught is the law of Moses, the same Law that the Spirit writes on our hearts.
- If we are led by the Spirit, we are enabled to carry out God's Law.

Led by the Spirit

Law and Spirit: Polar opposites, right? It seems that many consider this to be the case. Some suggest that obedience to the Torah (Law) does not allow for the leading of the Holy Spirit. However, Scripture indicates that one of the Spirit's main purposes in our lives is to enable us to walk according to the Law.

We read in the book of Acts about the believers' miraculous encounters with the Spirit of God. But the Holy Spirit had been moving, operating, and changing the lives of people from the very beginning. The Hebrew Scriptures teach us about certain heroes, long before the book of Acts, who were full of the same Holy Spirit. The Spirit of the Lord did not teach them to disobey the Torah of Moses.

In fact, Moses himself bore the Holy Spirit. It is the Holy Spirit that instructed and guided Moses to write and teach the people the Torah. The Sinai Law itself is a work of the revelation of the Holy Spirit. And Moses was not the only one with the Holy Spirit in those days. God explained to him that he would take some of the Spirit that was upon him and place it upon the elders of the children of Israel.[12]

Was this done so that they could live outside the "letter of the Law" and teach the people to disobey the Torah's written regulations? No. The Spirit of God enabled them to make judgments concerning God's holy Law, to apply it accurately, and to teach it to the Israelites. The Holy Spirit enlightened their eyes to understand and apply the Torah of Moses. The Spirit still does this for us.

The Lord declared that Moses' successor, Joshua, was full of the Spirit.[13] Did this Spirit-filled man feel that being bound to the Mosaic Law curtailed his ability to follow the Spirit's leading? No. The beginning of the book of Joshua reveals that the Spirit of God instructed and encouraged Joshua to obey the Torah:

> Only be strong and very courageous, being careful to do according to all the law [Torah] that Moses my servant commanded you. Do not turn from it to the right hand or to the left, that you may have good success wherever you go. This Book of the Law [Torah] shall not depart from your mouth, but you shall meditate on it day and night, so that you may be careful to do according to all that is written in it. For then you will make your way prosperous, and then you will have good success. (Joshua 1:7–8)

Certainly Joshua heeded the Spirit's instruction, for he instructed the children of Israel, saying,

Only be very careful to observe the commandment and the law [Torah] that Moses the servant of the LORD commanded you, to love the LORD your God, and to walk in all his ways and to keep his commandments and to cling to him and to serve him with all your heart and with all your soul. (Joshua 22:5)

This type of guidance is what God's Spirit has always given.

The Promise of the Prophets

Some might suggest that the aforementioned passages are irrelevant since they speak to an earlier dispensation. However, God promised through the prophets that he would send us the Spirit at the time of the ultimate redemption and the New Covenant, and that the Spirit would transform our hearts and lives. For example, Jeremiah speaks of the work of the Holy Spirit in the New Covenant era when he says,

"But this is the covenant that I will make with the house of Israel after those days," declares the LORD: "I will put my law [Torah] within them, and I will write it on their hearts. And I will be their God, and they shall be my people." (Jeremiah 31:33)

One common interpretation of this verse is that the Law "within them" and "on their hearts" was a different Law then than it is now. According to this reckoning, since the heart is a living medium, the Law is also changeable and adaptable rather than rigid and inflexible. One might suggest from this that the Torah commands are dictated by an ambiguous inner voice rather than being clearly engraved on stone or penned on parchment.

However, such an interpretation ignores the Hebraic symbolism that the prophet employed. Although in Western thought the heart is the source of emotion, the Bible speaks of the heart

The commandments, "love the LORD your God" and "love your neighbor," are direct quotes from the Mosaic Law.

as the locus of our decision-making process, akin to the mind. It is our will, where we process judgments.

Thus, to have the Torah written on our hearts means that it becomes so ingrained into our decision-making process that we never deviate from it. It is a part of our programming. This common Hebrew idiom can be seen elsewhere in Scripture.[14] So although there is a change that occurs with the advent of the New Covenant, the change is not in the Law but in our ability to carry it out effectively.

In fact, one of the main promises of the New Covenant is that the Holy Spirit empowers us to live out the Torah:

> And I will give you a new heart, and a new spirit I will put within you. And I will remove the heart of stone from your flesh and give you a heart of flesh. And I will put my Spirit within you, and cause you to walk in my statutes and be careful to obey my rules. (Ezekiel 36:26–27)

What does it mean that he will "write it on our heart"? It means that the Holy Spirit transforms our will to conform to the Torah of God.

What about Pentecost?

Acts 2 tells the story of the Spirit of God being poured out upon many people. This occurred during the pilgrimage festival of Pentecost, known in Hebrew as Shavu'ot.[15] (Jewish teaching associates this festival with the miraculous giving of the Law on Mount Sinai.) One purpose of this mass outpouring was to empower believers to be witnesses of the risen Messiah and the good news of the Kingdom of God. In addition, believers in Jesus were granted access to some of the promises described in the prophecies about the New Covenant.

By the power of his Spirit, God also transforms us in the way he promised in Jeremiah and Ezekiel, just as he did with the first-century followers of Jesus. He gives us new energy and the ability to carry out the Torah. This is the message of the outpouring at Pentecost.

The Same Law

And what about the writings of the prophets? Some say that the statutes and ordinances of which the prophets speak do not represent the law of Moses, but rather the law of Christ. They explain that the law of Christ brings an end to the law of Moses and does not involve lists of specific regulations. They suggest that the law of Christ says only, "Love God, and love one another."

But the commandments "love the LORD your God" and "love your neighbor" are direct quotes from the Mosaic law.[16] The law Jesus quotes is simply a summary of the Torah, not a replacement of it. Similarly, Joshua (as quoted previously) seemed to believe that "love God" summarized the Torah of Moses. Jewish sages before and after the days of Jesus' earthly ministry have always declared that "love God" and "love your neighbor" are the central teachings of the Hebrew Scriptures.

The commandments given on the mountain, scribed by the very finger of God, are inspired by the Holy Spirit. The Holy Spirit is God himself, and God does not change. When he gave the holy statutes and laws to Israel, he did not make up random, insignificant, or arbitrary rules. Rather, every commandment reveals his precise will and accurately shows what God values and considers important. The God who gave his Law to Moses is the same God who sent his Son, Jesus. The Spirit that filled Moses is the same Spirit that filled the apostles. What God considers right and good has not and will not change, and it is revealed in the Torah.

If God's condemnation of sinners is based on their failure to meet the standard of righteousness found in the Mosaic law, then that same standard of righteousness becomes the ultimate goal of the transforming work of the Holy Spirit. There cannot be two definitions of right and wrong. God does not have two different standards of righteousness.

The Torah warns that if a man claims to be a prophet but teaches people to stray from the commandments that Moses taught, then he is a false prophet.[17] From this we learn that the Messiah must uphold and teach the Torah, which he does:

> Therefore whoever relaxes one of the least of these commandments and teaches others to do the same will be called least in the kingdom of heaven, but whoever does them and teaches them will be called great in the kingdom of heaven. (Matthew 5:19)

Not under the Law

People often suggest that the Spirit enables a person to break the Torah. For example, one might cite, "If you are led by the Spirit, you are not under the law" (Galatians 5:18). However, to interpret being "under the law" as refering to scrupulous observance of the commandments denies the context of the passage. The passage states that the opposite of the Spirit is the flesh, which cannot produce lawful observance; rather, the flesh breaks the Law. This verse reiterates the statement two verses back: "But I say, walk by the Spirit, and you will not gratify the desires of the flesh" (Galatians 5:16).

Is the desire of the flesh to obey the commandments of God? Of course not. The deeds of the flesh are acts of disobedience: "sexual immorality, impurity, sensuality, idolatry, sorcery, enmity, strife, jealousy, fits of anger, rivalries, dissensions, divisions, envy, drunkenness, orgies, and things like these" (Galatians 5:19–21). If the Spirit and the flesh are at odds with one another, and if walking in the flesh produces disobedience to God's Torah, then walking in the Spirit will produce obedience. Thus, being "led by the Spirit" means accepting the Holy Spirit's promptings to walk in the commandments of the Torah.

What then does being "under the law" mean? The letter to the Galatians is not against obeying the Torah; it's against using the ritual of conversion (circumcision) to become Jewish as a means of salvation. The ones relying on the conversion ritual are the ones "under the law." As Paul notes in the next chapter of Galatians, those people were not even observing the Torah; they were relying on their Jewish legal status for acceptance before God and men.[18] He speaks against this, saying, "Neither circumcision [i.e., legal status as a Jewish person] counts for anything nor uncircumcision [i.e., legal status as a Gentile], but keeping the commandments of God" (1 Corinthians 7:19).[19] To be "under the law" does not mean being obedient to the commandments but to use one's supposed legal Jewish status to give an excuse to sin.

Ultimately, Scripture says that the Spirit causes us to obey the Torah. "Love God and love one another" is a summary of all of the commandments. By observing them with a pure heart and the renewing work of the Spirit, we live out that love.

> Whoever keeps his commandments abides in God, and God in him. And by this we know that he abides in us, by the Spirit whom he has given us. (1 John 3:24)

Torah and Spirit Are Not Opposites

And I will put my Spirit within you, and cause you to walk in my statutes and be careful to obey my rules. (Ezekiel 36:27)

The Spirit of God that spoke the commandments of the Law is the same Spirit that came upon the believers at Pentecost in Acts 2. The prophets predicted that in the New Covenant, God's Spirit would lead us to obey his commandments and would write his Law on our hearts. This is the same Law that God gave through Moses at Mount Sinai. Therefore, the Spirit and the Law are not opposites. Instead, the leading of the Spirit causes us and enables us to carry out the commandments of God's Law.

Discipleship Is Imitation

Key Points

- As the ultimate prophet and king, Jesus taught and observed every detail of the Law.
- The responsibility of a disciple is to imitate his teacher.
- Disciples of Jesus would do well to follow his example of obedience to the commandments of the Law.

Walking as He Walked

Was Jesus really Torah observant? Classic interpretations of the Messiah often paint him as a free-spirited fellow who encouraged people not to be so strict with their obedience. Reducing the commandments of God to general niceness, he is portrayed as not too concerned with what the biblical Law specifically says.

Some go so far as to suggest that Jesus didn't even obey the commandments himself. From their reading of the Gospels, they deduce that Jesus broke the Sabbath laws, ate foods that the Torah prohibits (i.e., food that is not kosher), and disregarded the biblical ritual purity laws.[20]

However, we know that this cannot be true. Jesus must have been strictly obedient to the smallest detail of the biblical Law, or else he would have been a sinner. As a sinner, he certainly could not be our Savior. His death would have meant nothing to us, since he would have died in his own sin. He would have been just like any other man.

Yet we know from his teachings that he was strictly obedient to the Torah. He declares,

> Do not think that I have come to abolish the Law or the Prophets; I have not come to abolish them but to fulfill them. For truly, I say to you, until heaven and earth pass away, not an iota, not a dot, will pass from the Law until all is accomplished. (Matthew 5:17–18)

Some who read this passage interpret the word *fulfill* to mean that these commandments have come to an end. However, this effectively means the same thing as "abolish," rendering the passage self-contradictory. Perhaps all was accomplished at the crucifixion or at the resurrection. No, this cannot be true either, since heaven and earth have not yet passed away. Besides, there is more for Messiah to accomplish in his second coming.[21]

But Jesus doesn't stop there. He instructs us further, saying,

> Therefore whoever relaxes one of the least of these commandments and teaches others to do the same will be called least in the kingdom of heaven, but whoever does them and teaches them will be called great in the kingdom of heaven. (Matthew 5:19)

If Jesus broke the commandments in the Torah, or if he instructed others to do so, he would have condemned himself by this very statement. Instead, if we understand his deeds and teachings in light of this verse, then we will find that Jesus upheld the Law in every respect. In fact, the very Scriptures that prophesy about the coming of the Messiah declare that he would do so.

The Ultimate Prophet

According to the litmus test the Israelites were given to see if a prophet was really from God, the Messiah is the ultimate prophet.[22] If any supposed prophet told people to break the commandments, then he was not to be obeyed, as Scripture says,

> If a prophet or a dreamer of dreams arises among you and gives you a sign or a wonder, and the sign or wonder that he tells you comes to pass, and if he says, "Let us go after other gods," which you have not known, "and let us serve them," you shall not listen to the words of that prophet or that dreamer of dreams. For the LORD your God is testing you, to know whether you love the LORD your God with all your heart and with all your soul. You shall walk after the LORD your God and fear him and keep his commandments and obey his voice, and you shall serve him and hold fast to him. But that prophet or that dreamer of dreams shall be put to death, because he has taught rebellion against the LORD your God, who brought you out of the land of Egypt and redeemed you out of the house of slavery, to make you leave the way in which the LORD your God commanded you to walk. So you shall purge the evil from your midst. (Deuteronomy 13:1–5)

Many Orthodox Jews who reject Jesus do so largely on account of this passage. But this is because Jesus has been portrayed incorrectly. For centuries, historical Christianity has portrayed Jesus and his teachings in opposition to the Jewish people and the Mosaic Law. As a result of this false portrayal (accompanied by severe persecution at the hand of Christians), some observant Jews conceive of Jesus in a similar way to arch-villains in Jewish and biblical history, such as Pharaoh and Haman. The blame for this tragic misunderstanding cannot simply be placed

> Our rightstanding before God is based on the
> righteousness that was lived out by our Master;
> it is wrong to use his grace as an excuse to sin.

on Jewish "blindness"; Christians must consider the implications of their theology, message, and behavior.

Contrary to this portrayal, as the ultimate prophet of God, Jesus really did live out the commandments, and like the other prophets, he called people to turn back to God's Law in repentance as well.

The Ultimate King

Not only is the Messiah the ultimate prophet, but he is the ultimate king of Israel. The biblical Law also gives rules regarding the acceptance of Israel's king:

> And when he sits on the throne of his kingdom, he
> shall write for himself in a book a copy of this law
> [Torah], approved by the Levitical priests. And it shall
> be with him, and he shall read in it all the days of his
> life, that he may learn to fear the LORD his God by
> keeping all the words of this law [Torah] and these
> statutes, and doing them, that his heart may not be
> lifted up above his brothers, and that he may not
> turn aside from the commandment, either to the
> right hand or to the left, so that he may continue
> long in his kingdom, he and his children, in Israel.
> (Deuteronomy 17:18–20)

Jesus must be strictly observant of the Law of God in order to qualify as king of Israel, as defined by the Bible. In fact, prophecies concerning the coming messiah clearly state that he will establish observance of biblical Law. For example, the prophet Ezekiel tells us about the future kingship of the messiah when he says, "My servant David shall be king over them, and they shall all have one shepherd. They shall walk in my rules and be careful to obey my statutes" (Ezekiel 37:24).[23]

Discipleship

Although he is perhaps the most well known for having disciples, Jesus did not invent the concept of discipleship. This rigorous method of training was an institution that was well in place by the time he began his ministry. The call of discipleship in first-century Judaism was much more than Bible schooling. A rabbi taught his disciples how to live every aspect of life.

The job of a disciple was to imitate his teacher in every way, learning not only the way he understood Scripture but also how he ate, how he celebrated holidays, how he gave charity, and every detail of his life. The Master himself explains, "A disciple is not above his teacher, but everyone when he is fully trained will be like his teacher" (Luke 6:40).

As twenty-first-century disciples of Jesus, our task is still to learn to imitate him in every way. We know two important things about him: He obeyed the biblical Law, even to the smallest detail, and he taught others to do the same. If the Messiah, Son of God and King of Israel, humbled himself in obedience to the commandments of the Torah, shouldn't we? Or do we consider ourselves greater than our Master?

Our mission is to determine how to imitate the Messiah's actions in our lives. This includes how we care for others and how we pray, as well as how we eat and celebrate. Jesus instructed us to obey even the smallest detail of the Torah.[24] The commandments of the biblical Law are the commandments of Jesus himself.

A common objection arises at this point: "Jesus also didn't use a microwave or drive a car! Does that mean we should walk everywhere and cook everything over an open flame?" Based on examples of advancement in civilization or technology, many conclude that it is futile to even try to imitate our Master's observance of the commandments. At times such hypothetical questions are simply ways to avoid being accountable to walk after him to the best of our ability. When we examine what he did in the context of his surroundings, we find many ways to imitate him by living a life of faithfulness to God in today's world.

Others explain, "He did it so we don't have to." However, there are many commandments that Jesus did not perform because they did not apply to him. Since he did not observe laws for women regarding menstruation, does this mean these laws remain unfulfilled? By the same logic, it would be acceptable to rape, murder, and steal, since he "fulfilled" the whole Law.

Our right standing before God is based on the righteousness that was lived out by our Master; it is wrong to use his grace as an excuse to sin. We don't obey the Torah because we "have to" but because he did and we want to follow his example.

The Apostle John learned about true discipleship firsthand. He explains:

> And by this we know that we have come to know him, if we keep his commandments. Whoever says "I know him" but does not keep his commandments is a liar, and the truth is not in him, but whoever keeps his word, in him truly the love of God is perfected. By this we may know that we are in him: whoever says he abides in him ought to walk in the same way in which he walked. (1 John 2:3–6)

BOUNDARY STONE

Discipleship Is Imitation

A disciple is not above his teacher, but everyone when he is fully trained will be like his teacher. (Luke 6:40)

Keeping the Law is part of discipleship to Jesus, because Jesus was a Torah-observant Jew. As the ultimate prophet and king over Israel, Jesus taught the Law and observed every detail of the Law that applied to him. If he did not, he would not qualify as the Messiah. Jesus calls his followers to walk after him as his disciples. The responsibility of a disciple is to imitate his teacher. Therefore, disciples of Jesus would do well to follow his example.

God Does Not Change

Key Points

- The idea that God and his expectations change is dangerous and inaccurate.
- God is a good and consistent father.
- God's expectations have not changed.

The Unchanging God

In the second century AD, the first attempt was made to form an official Christian canon of Scripture. A man named Marcion of Sinope formed a list of the books that he considered to be the true word of God. It consisted only of ten of Paul's letters and a carefully edited version of the gospel of Luke.

To Marcion, the Scriptures of Judaism were off limits because he was heavily influenced by Gnosticism,[25] which taught that the Old Testament God was a different deity altogether from the God of the New Testament. The New Testament God as revealed by Jesus is loving and gracious, but the Old Testament God was vindictive and wrathful. To Marcion, Jesus did not come to fulfill messianic prophecies spoken by the Jewish prophets but to herald a new religion and proclaim a new and better god.

Naturally, many church fathers rejected Marcion for his extreme beliefs, formally excommunicating him. They ultimately accepted the Hebrew Scriptures into the Bible and affirmed a historical and theological connection to Judaism.

Marcion was marginalized, but ideas similar to his continue influencing people to believe that obedience to the Hebrew Scriptures is incompatible with faith in Jesus as the Messiah. And there are some who continue to believe that Paul's letters or the New Testament are all that are needed in order to know and understand God. Underlying this is the subconscious conviction that God is somehow different now than he used to be. In their minds, God has changed.

God Does Not Change

> Of old you laid the foundation of the earth, and the heavens are the work of your hands. They will perish, but you will remain; they will all wear out like a garment. You will change them like a robe, and they will pass away, but you are the same, and your years have no end. (Psalm 102:25–27)

The idea of a changing God is incompatible with Scripture. In fact, the Bible emphasizes God's enduring and consistent nature. It is one major feature that distinguishes him from false gods.

For example, even God's personal name reveals his consistency. In Exodus 6, God indicates that he made himself known to the patriarchs as El Shaddai ("All-Sufficient God" or "Almighty God"), but he did not make himself known to them as the LORD.[26] This is curious, since it is clear that Abraham, Isaac, and Jacob did indeed know this name of God.

God's dialogue with Moses at the burning bush shows that God is called by this name because, as he declares, "I am who I am" (Exodus 3:14). The Hebrew of this phrase[27] carries the sense of "I will continue to be who I will continue to be." It describes God's consistent character. This consistent character was not made known to the fathers; while they did receive the promises of God, they did not experience their fulfillment. The fulfillment was revealed through Moses, thereby finally demonstrating God's unchanging nature and thus exemplifying the meaning of his personal name. God's personal name indicates his consistency and devotion to covenant. As the book of Malachi indicates, "For I the LORD do not change; therefore you, O children of Jacob, are not consumed" (Malachi 3:6).

A Loving Father

> I said, "How I would set you among my sons, and give you a pleasant land, a heritage most beautiful of all nations." And I thought you would call me, "My Father," and would not turn from following me. (Jeremiah 3:19)

God is revealed throughout Scripture as Israel's loving father. He says as much in the Torah when redeeming Israel from Pharaoh,[28] giving laws of holiness,[29] and correcting their error.[30] This theme continues throughout the Scriptures.[31]

Imagine an earthly father who was inconsistent with his children. He would give his children a set of rules, and at a certain point he would punish them severely for breaking them. Then, once they had learned to follow his new directions, he would suddenly change the rules again, instructing them to disregard his previous commands. If they broke his new laws, he would punish them even more severely than before by disowning them and sending them away. Would this be a just, merciful, and good father? Obviously not.

Yet this is the implication of what some have taught about God and his commandments. Israel, whom God calls his first-born son, suffered in punishment, exile, famine, and war. Thousands upon thousands of people of Israel have been removed from their homes or put to the sword throughout the centuries. The prophets explicitly indicate that this severe punishment is from God their father because they have broken his Torah. And so they entreat Israel to return to his Law.

Therefore, as the tongue of fire devours the stubble, and as dry grass sinks down in the flame, so their root will be as rottenness, and their blossom go up like dust; for they have rejected the law [Torah] of the LORD of hosts, and have despised the word of the Holy One of Israel. (Isaiah 5:24)[32]

When Jesus came, did he bring in a new era in which we no longer need to obey the Mosaic Law? Are there new laws for us to obey?

If there are, then the chastisement that Israel endured generation after generation was for nothing. From this perspective, our only conclusion can be that either God has changed or that he hated Israel.

Justin Martyr, one of the early Christian apologists, rejected Marcion's idea of a new god, but he explained that God imposed the Mosaic laws (particularly the Sabbath and circumcision) upon the Jews as a punishment for their stiff-necked wickedness.[33] To Justin Martyr these were signs that the Jews were to bear, like Hitler's yellow badges, so that people would know who the "Christ killers" were.

It is a common teaching throughout church history that God punished the Jews before Christ came because they broke the Law, and punished the Jews after Christ came because they rejected Jesus and kept the Law. It should not be surprising, then, to hear central church figures such as John Chrysostom, St. Augustine, and even respected reformers such as Martin Luther and John Calvin, expressing sentiments of hatred for the Jewish people.

What can we do? Can we tolerate a doctrine that leads to that kind of hate? It would seem that in order for anti-Semitic sentiment to be quenched in the church, anti-Torah sentiment must also be quenched. If we understand the Torah as loving instruction from a father to his children, then we will under-

The idea of a changing God is incompatible with Scripture.

stand how Israel should be treated. Followers of Jesus can begin rebuilding the road to reconciliation.

God's Word Does Not Change

"Forever, O LORD, your word is firmly fixed in the heavens" (Psalm 119:89). We must recognize our Father's consistency. He does not change, nor do his expectations of us. His Word remains the same.

The instructions found in God's Torah are a gift for those who have received his grace. Obedience to his commandments is beneficial to us. As Psalm 19:7 tells us, "The law [Torah] of the LORD is perfect, reviving the soul." The Hebrew word for "perfect" is *temimah*, meaning "whole, lacking nothing."

Just as God does not change, the Torah of God, his expressed will for humanity, will endure forever. Just as God is perfect, his commandments are "holy and righteous and good" (Romans 7:12), without need for improvement. They are whole, complete, and lack nothing.

As sons and daughters of God, let's renew our commitment to his loving instruction, which is eternal.

BOUNDARY STONE

God Does Not Change

God is not man, that he should lie, or a son of man, that he should change his mind. (Numbers 23:19)

Depicting God as if he capriciously changes his mind about things is theologically dangerous. God is eternal and unchanging. And if he does not change, then neither do the expectations that he spelled out for us in his Law. God does not reverse His word or arbitrarily suspend his commandments, punishing his people for what he once praised them and praising them for what he once punished them. Instead, he is a good and consistent father, the same yesterday, today, and forever.

Scripture Cannot Contradict the Law

Key Points

- Scripture as a whole presents the Law as an eternal standard of godly living—not as a lesson to be discarded at a later time.

- Paul's view of the Law does not conflict with the rest of the Bible.

- Paul's message is about Gentiles putting their faith in Jesus, granting them adoption into Israel and bringing them near to the Law, its blessings, and commandments.

The Complete Testimony of Scripture

Is adherence to the Torah a worthwhile goal for those who put our faith in Jesus, or is it utter futility? It might seem that the case is closed. It is a common impression to believe that Scripture relegates the Torah to an obsolete object lesson.

However, people generally find support for this view within only a few of the letters of Paul. The initial response to a Torah-promoting message is often "What about Galatians?" or "What about Romans?" Rarely are the words of Deuteronomy, Isaiah, Matthew, or James brought into the picture. Nonetheless, these are valid questions. Our task is to seek to understand the message of each book by reading it in the context of history and the rest of Scripture.

One important issue with the passages frequently cited from Paul is the apparent discrepancy between them and the rest of Scripture. Can an interpretation of Paul be correct if it contradicts other parts of the Bible? Following are supposed examples of such biblical conflict.

Moses

In Deuteronomy 13:1–5, Moses warns Israel that even a miracle worker who tells them to neglect the commandments of the Law is a false prophet sent by God to test them. Moses says that a prophet or seer who attempts to dissuade the people from keeping God's commandments is to be put to death.

To put this in contemporary terms, suppose you were recently hired as a security guard in a large manufacturing plant. You were given strict orders not to allow anyone to enter the facility between eleven o'clock at night and five o'clock in the morning under any circumstances. During your training for the position, you were informed of a scam in which people would dress in the company uniform and present forged IDs in order to gain illicit entrance to the building at night. If a person attempts to enter the building after hours, the employee handbook explicitly states that the person should be arrested for trespassing, regardless of the credentials they present.

Lo and behold, on the very first night on duty, a man shows up in company uniform, presenting his authentic-looking identification and requesting entry. You explain to him that you cannot grant him entrance since the employee handbook explicitly states that no one may enter after hours.

He responds with a surprising answer: "I know, I know. But the CEO himself told me to tell you that I have his direct permission. What's more important—the company handbook or the word of the CEO himself? Besides, that rule has outlived its purpose since the perpetrators of that scam have all been caught. Didn't you hear about that?"

Of course, if you are a wise security guard, you will not let him enter. He could very well be a con artist seeking to gain unauthorized access. Perhaps he was even sent by your supervisors to test your competence in your new position. On the off-chance that this person seeking entrance is legitimate, you would be dealing with a very irresponsible employer.

If either Jesus or Paul declared an end to the Law, the above scenario would illustrate the position of the Jewish people who first heard their message. Would God give them a command to execute one who leads them away from the Torah—and then send Paul to tell them that they are free from the Law? We are left with a few logical conclusions:

a) Paul was the false prophet God warned about in Deuteronomy 13.

b) God is forgetful, malicious, and incoherent.

c) The book of Galatians and Paul's teaching about the Torah have been misunderstood.

This is not the only aspect of the Torah that presents a problem. Moses also made clear that renewed observance of the Law would accompany the future redemption. "And you shall again obey the voice of the LORD and keep all his commandments that I command you today" (Deuteronomy 30:8).

The Prophets

The prophets warned Israel not to stray from the Law. When they did, they encountered severe punishment, including loss of life.[34] The prophets repeated the promise of redemption accompanied by observance.[35] It is impossible to reconcile this with an interpretation of Paul that the Messiah came to free us from the Law.

If [Paul] had believed the Torah had been put to an end, then this would have been the perfect time to speak up.

Psalms and Proverbs

The Psalms and Proverbs constantly extol the virtues of the Torah, not merely as a tool to point to the Messiah but as an eternal handbook for righteous living. Not only is the Torah pure and perfect,[36] but it is equated with fear of God, which "endures forever."[37] The psalmists declare that it is the delight of the righteous person,[38] residing in his heart.[39] Those who practice it are "blessed."[40] The inspired writers of these texts uphold it as a permanent standard of righteousness.[41] The psalmist declares its eternal purpose plainly:

> He established a testimony in Jacob and appointed a law [Torah] in Israel, which he commanded our fathers to teach to their children, that the next generation might know them, the children yet unborn, and arise and tell them to their children, so that they should set their hope in God and not forget the works of God, but keep his commandments; and that they should not be like their fathers, a stubborn and rebellious generation, a generation whose heart was not steadfast, whose spirit was not faithful to God. (Psalm 78:5–8)

These truths conflict with an interpretation of Paul that the Torah can be dismissed.

Jesus' Teaching

Jesus gave no indication that observance of the Law should end. Instead, he said:

> Therefore whoever relaxes one of the least of these commandments and teaches others to do the same will be called least in the kingdom of heaven, but whoever does them and teaches them will be called great in the kingdom of heaven. (Matthew 5:19)

Certainly Paul will not be called least in God's kingdom.

Acts

James and the elders glorified God because thousands of believers were "zealous for the law" (Acts 21:20). Paul had been accused of teaching "all the Jews who are among the Gentiles to forsake Moses, telling them not to circumcise their children or walk according to our customs" (Acts 21:21). To disprove this accusation, Paul was instructed to provide Nazarite offerings for some of the believers present in Jerusalem, so that "all will know that there is nothing in what they have been told about you, but that you yourself also live in observance of the law" (Acts 21:24).

The vow of the Nazarite is described in Numbers 6:1–21. When one finishes the term of his Nazarite vow, he is required to present an offering: one male lamb, one female lamb, and one ram, in addition to a substantial amount of unleavened bread, grain, oil, and wine. In this instance, there were four Nazarites for whom Paul would provide a total of twelve sacrificial animals—no small expense! If he had believed the Torah had been put to an end, then this would have been the perfect time to speak up. Instead, the writer of Acts reports,

> Then Paul took the men, and the next day he purified himself along with them and went into the temple,

giving notice when the days of purification would
be fulfilled and the offering presented for each one
of them. (Acts 21:26)

Other Epistles

The epistles of James, Peter, and John repeatedly uphold observance of the Law and make no mention of it having outlived
its usefulness. James explains, "But the one who looks into the
perfect law, the law of liberty, and perseveres, being no hearer
who forgets but a doer who acts, he will be blessed in his doing"
(James 1:25).

The "perfect law" is the law of Moses.[42] The "law of liberty"
is James's loving term for the law of Moses; he indicates that the
"law of liberty" contains the commandments "Do not commit
adultery" and "Do not murder."[43]

Peter points out that Paul's letters are "hard to understand"
(2 Peter 3:16), but the error of misunderstanding is committed by those who are "lawless" (2 Peter 3:17).[44] The Greek word
translated "lawless" is *athesmos* (a different word from *anomia*),
which literally means "against law/custom."

The epistles of John explain,

> And by this we know that we have come to know
> him, if we keep his commandments. Whoever says "I
> know him" but does not keep his commandments is
> a liar, and the truth is not in him, but whoever keeps
> his word, in him truly the love of God is perfected. By
> this we may know that we are in him: whoever says
> he abides in him ought to walk in the same way in
> which he walked. (1 John 2:3–6)

As previously discussed, the "way [Jesus] walked" was in
full and perfect obedience to the commandments in the law of
Moses. This epistle also equates breaking the Law with sin:

Everyone who makes a practice of sinning also practices lawlessness; sin is lawlessness. You know that he appeared to take away sins, and in him there is no sin. No one who abides in him keeps on sinning; no one who keeps on sinning has either seen him or known him. Little children, let no one deceive you. Whoever practices righteousness is righteous, as he is righteous. (1 John 3:4–7)

Furthermore, 1 John indicates that love of God is manifested through obedience to his commandments:

By this we know that we love the children of God, when we love God and obey his commandments. For this is the love of God, that we keep his commandments. And his commandments are not burdensome. (1 John 5:2–3)

Even the book of Revelation identifies the children of the woman as "those who keep the commandments of God and hold to the testimony of Jesus" (Revelation 12:17) and the saints as those "who keep the commandments of God and their faith in Jesus" (14:12).

Paul's Own Writings

The discrepancy reaches even into Paul's own writings:

For it is not the hearers of the law who are righteous before God, but the doers of the law who will be justified. (Romans 2:13)

So, if a man who is uncircumcised keeps the precepts of the law, will not his uncircumcision be regarded as circumcision? Then he who is physically uncircumcised but keeps the law will condemn you who have the written code and circumcision but break the law. (Romans 2:26–27)

Do we then overthrow the law by this faith? By no means! On the contrary, we uphold the law. (Romans 3:31)

For neither circumcision counts for anything nor uncircumcision, but keeping the commandments of God. (1 Corinthians 7:19)

When compared against the whole counsel of Scripture, passages that appear to diminish the importance of Torah seem out of place. This becomes especially clear when we try to gain the worldview of the original recipients and to read the Bible in the context of first-century Judaism.

Paul the Heretic?

Did Paul so casually cast off the foundational revelation of God as a relic of a bygone era? The thousands of years of history and theology that have transpired since then have desensitized us to how scandalous that idea actually is. If this was Paul's message, then it was not just a new covenant or a new era he was describing, but a new Bible, a new religion, and an entirely new god. The interpretation of Paul as one opposed to Torah observance is simply incompatible with the faith of Moses and Jesus. Either Paul is wrong or the conventional reading of Paul is wrong.

Is it possible that Paul could be so misunderstood? Some hints, as previously mentioned, give us clues. In Acts 21, people mistakenly believed that Paul taught against the law of Moses and Jewish custom. Paul refuted that misconception by cooperating with James and the elders in keeping Torah law regarding the Nazarites.

2 Peter 3:16 explains that Paul's letters are "hard to understand" and that the true error is to be against law/custom. It is easy for Paul to be misunderstood, and, according to these passages, if we understand Paul as teaching people to disobey

Paul was dealing with Gentiles who were
insecure in their identity.

the law of Moses and Jewish custom, then we are in fact misunderstanding him.

So What Does Paul Mean?

The central issue in all of the letters of Paul is the same, and it
is not observance of the Law or Jewish custom, per se. It is the
same issue that is pivotal in the book of Acts: the inclusion of
Gentiles in the kingdom of God.

Today we take for granted that Gentiles can come to God
and be acceptable to him without first becoming Jewish in a
legal sense through a ritual conversion. We are so used to that
idea, we can't imagine it any other way. In the apostolic era,
however, that was a very contentious issue and a hard thing
for many to accept.

Jesus is the Messiah of Judaism; he is the Messiah of the
Jewish people. If people want to follow him, it is reasoned that
they must first convert and become like him: Jewish. This was
the prevailing opinion of many believers in the apostolic community. Through Peter's experience in the middle of the book
of Acts, he learned that Gentiles could remain Gentiles and still
enter the kingdom. Nonetheless, this idea was so shocking to
people (including even Peter at first) that it remained a topic of
fierce debate. This is the main issue of Paul's letters as well as
the book of Acts.

People were teaching the Galatian community that they had
to convert and become legally Jewish to be included in God's
kingdom. Paul's letter to them was intended to dispel that belief.
For example, Paul uses the terms *circumcision* and *uncircumcision* repeatedly. It is tempting to interpret these literally as a

medical procedure; however, these were technical terms for "being/becoming Jewish" versus "remaining Gentile." In fact, this is often how the terms are used in rabbinic writings. This idea might also be reflected in his term "under law."

Paul was dealing with Gentiles who were insecure in their identity. They had the impression that as Gentiles who did not keep the Torah, they were specifically subject to God's condemnation. They believed that if they became Jews through conversion, they could automatically escape that condemnation and still live contrary to Torah. Some (particularly those addressed in Romans) had already gone through that conversion, pointing fingers at the ones who had not.[45]

Paul refuted them by explaining that people with a legal Jewish status do not escape punishment.[46] In fact, he points out, they are subject to even more swift and strict judgment because they formally acknowledged their obligation to keep the commandments.[47] Thus, becoming Jewish through legal conversion does not deflect judgment from someone who violates the Torah as they might hope; it actually invites and intensifies that judgment.[48]

Taking Paul Seriously

This reading of Paul not only stands in harmony with all of Scripture, but has substantial implications for Gentiles who follow Jesus. If we take Paul's message seriously, then we understand that our salvation through Messiah does not distance us from the Torah, but it actually grants Gentiles who put faith in him access to share in the blessings, covenants, promises, heritage, and commandments God revealed through the Jewish people. Paul teaches that Gentiles are included in God's kingdom through faith in Jesus in order to serve him obediently and to benefit from his goodness alongside the Jewish people.

BOUNDARY STONE
Scripture Cannot Contradict the Law

Do we then overthrow the law by this faith? By no means!
On the contrary, we uphold the law. (Romans 3:31)

All the scriptures in the Bible present the Law as an eternal standard of godly living—not a temporary lesson to be discarded at a later time. The Law is the foundation on which the rest of the Scriptures are built. If someone wrote something that contradicted or overturned the law of Moses, his writings could not be considered to be inspired scripture. Therefore, if Paul's writings contradict the law of Moses, they should not be included in the Bible. However, if Paul's message is about Gentile inclusion within God's people (Israel), then the Gentiles who put faith in Jesus are brought near to the people, blessings, covenants, and commandments of Israel.

The New Testament Cannot Overturn the Old

Key Points

- The Scriptures were revealed in stages, each stage building upon the previous revelation.
- The authority of the office of messiah is derived from the Hebrew Scriptures.
- Reading the Bible "backward" leads to problematic results.
- The Torah forms the core of our perspective and faith.

The Foundation of the Bible

The story of the Bible is fascinating. It did not drop out of heaven as a complete unit. It was neither discovered etched on golden tablets nor dictated beginning to end to a single prophet. Instead, God revealed it to mankind over hundreds of years in successive stages.

The first portion of the Bible to be revealed was the Torah. God gave the Torah to the Israelites through Moses and verified it audio-visually to millions of individuals at Mount Sinai. God established his authority by redeeming the Israelites from Egypt and then entered into covenant with them.

For some time, the five books of Moses constituted the only Bible anyone had. Nonetheless, God had worked into the Torah the ability (and inevitability) for additional revelation to come. The Torah specifically covers the topic of prophets in Deuteronomy chapters 13 and 18. Certainly an impostor could claim to be a prophet from God while leading Israel astray through false words. There had to be some way for the Israelites to be certain whether a prophet was from God.

One criterion seems obvious: If the prophet gives a prophecy that does not come to pass, then he is a false prophet (Deuteronomy 18:21–22). But what if the prophet demonstrates his power with some kind of miraculous sign? Although this might be tempting as evidence for divine backing, the Torah does not consider such a display as validating prophet credentials (Deuteronomy 13:1). The Torah does not even question whether the sign was a scientifically explainable hoax or an authentic supernatural event.

Instead, the final criterion for a true prophet is that he will not lead people to rebel against God, disobey his commandments, or turn from the way God showed them (Deuteronomy 13:2–5).

Thus, the Torah set a precedent whereby each successive wave of revelation would be tested by the revelation that came before. As each prophet or teacher came to Israel, his words were tested against the testimony of the Torah. The authenticity of each revelation was verified through comparison with each of the previous stages.

The Basis of Authority

By the time of Jesus' ministry, wise and godly Jewish men had established a collection of books proven divine in origin. (Esther and Song of Songs were added a little later.) These formed the Scriptures that the original disciples, Jesus, and his contemporaries knew. They were organized into three parts: the Torah, the Prophets, and the Writings (this included Psalms and the books of Chronicles, for example). This collection became known to Judaism as the Tanach[49] and to Christians as the Old Testament.

This ancient set of Scriptures revealed that a messiah would come. It is the authority of these previously validated prophecies that even allows someone to claim to be the messiah. Thus, the messiah's authority as a prophet, teacher, and king is founded upon the firmly established revelation of the Torah, the Prophets, and the Writings.

That is why the religious leaders of Jesus' time tested and questioned him. They had a right—even a responsibility—to do so as leaders of their faith communities. The Tanach is the standard by which they could rightly judge him. If he had not met its qualifications, if he had prophesied incorrectly, or if he had taught against obeying the Torah's instructions, then they would have been right in dismissing him as messiah, despite any miracles.

The Torah, the Prophets, and the Writings constitute a messiah's basis of authority. If a candidate for messiah were to dismiss or render obsolete any of that revelation—especially the Torah—he would undercut his own authority and render "messiah" a meaningless concept.

Fulfilling the Law

Jesus, of course, said that he did not "come to abolish the Law or the Prophets ... but to fulfill them" (Matthew 5:17). As we noted in chapter 5, one common misinterpretation of the term *fulfill* is that he satisfied all of its demands, thereby alleviating us from its constraints. This error paints the Torah like a complicated math problem or puzzle; once it's solved, it is no longer worth trying to solve again.

However, the Torah is not a problem waiting for a solution. There is no passage in the Torah that allows even a perfect indi-

*The final criterion for a true prophet is that he will
not lead people to rebel against God.*

vidual to escape its system or provide escape for others. The Torah never asks to be "fulfilled" in that sense.

This could be compared to a president of the United States. Near the end of his term, he declares that he has perfectly fulfilled every clause in the Constitution. Since he has done so, he announces that he is now free to put an end to the Constitution and establish a new system of government. Of course, his claim would be invalid for two reasons: First, the Constitution does not grant anyone a special status just because he does what he is supposed to do. Second, it is the Constitution that defines a president. If the Constitution is no longer in effect, then there is no such thing as the president anymore.

The authority of each prophet or teacher rests on the foundation of those who came beforehand. A teacher claiming to be from God, yet canceling or diminishing the first revelation, has undercut his own source of authority.

This applies not only to Jesus but to his disciples and apostles as well. Their teaching could not contradict the words of their master. Furthermore, since Jesus' teachings were based on the Tanach, they could not teach against the Torah, Prophets, or Writings either.

Reading the Bible Forward

The book of Acts praises the Jewish people in Berea. They did not simply accept Paul and Silas's words because they made a sign or wonder or claimed some kind of independent divine revelation. Nor did they accept them just because they followed someone whom they claimed rose from the dead or performed miracles. Instead, "These Jews were more noble than those in

Thessalonica; they received the word with all eagerness, examining the Scriptures daily to see if these things were so" (Acts 17:11).

Of course, the "Scriptures" they examined consisted only of the Tanach. If Paul or Silas had taught something in conflict with the Tanach, the Bereans would have flatly rejected them. These Berean Jews did the correct thing by beginning with the revelation that they had already received and building the message of the gospel upon it. The Torah, Prophets, and Writings formed the filter through which they discerned the truth of the gospel and interpreted its message.

This approach differs from "reading the Bible backward," which suggests that we should form our core perspectives from the New Testament first, because only then can we understand the true meaning and purpose of the Old Testament. Yet when the New Testament stands alone, it loses its context. The New Testament authors assumed that their readership was well acquainted with the Hebrew Scriptures, employing those symbols and allusions liberally and often without explanation. If we draw conclusions from the New Testament detached from its foundation, they are bound to be mistaken. Then, when the reader comes to the Tanach with mistaken assumptions, these conclusions will be artificially superimposed on the text.

A second issue with a "backward" perspective on Scripture is that it implies that one with a background in the Tanach would not naturally come to the conclusions found in the New Testament. It implies that what the New Testament contains about Jesus and redemption has to be assumed as true first, because a process of reasoned deduction would lead a person to believe otherwise. In some way this view seems to readily admit that the teachings of Jesus and the apostles depart from the inherently reasonable, face-value meaning of the Hebrew Scriptures.

In reality, if our theological assumptions are challenged by the plain meaning of God's Word, beginning with the Torah and moving forward, the correct response is to re-examine our perspectives, as painful as that might be. Our responsibility is to establish our own worldview primarily on the Torah, and then build upon that foundation with the rest of God's teaching. When we find teaching that does not seem to square with the Torah, it must be either false or misunderstood.

The Torah is permanently put in place by God as the foundation of the Scriptures. Jesus and his apostles were quite clearly masters of that text, and it formed the very core of their beliefs and their identity. Is the same true for us?

The New Testament Cannot Overturn the Old

All Scripture is breathed out by God and profitable for teaching, for reproof, for correction, and for training in righteousness.

(2 Timothy 3:16)

The Bible did not come in a box all at once. The Scriptures were revealed in successive stages over hundreds of years. Each stage of Scripture was built upon the previous ones. The law of Moses is the initial revelation of God and the oldest part of the Bible. It is the foundation for the rest of the Bible's books and the core revelation of biblical faith. The Prophets and Writings are built upon it; the Gospels and Apostolic Writings came last but built on the Law, the Prophets, and the Writings of the Old Testament.

The concept of messiah and the authority of that office are both derived from the earlier Scriptures of the Law and the Prophets and the Writings. Since the New Testament Scriptures base their authority on the Old Testament Scriptures, it is incorrect to read them as if they had more authority than the Law.

The Sabbath Is
an Eternal Covenant

Key Points

- God permanently infused the Sabbath with holiness and blessing at the time of creation.
- The Sabbath is a sign of eternal covenant between God and his people.
- The Sabbath testifies that the God of Israel is the only true God.
- The Sabbath provides a prophetic picture of our future eternal rest.

Ten Commandments

The Ten Commandments are important boundary stones for the Christian life. Most Christians agree that, at a minimum, we ought to keep the Ten Commandments. They include ethical commandments like prohibitions on idolatry, theft, adultery, murder, and false testimony. The only one that seems to be met with ambivalence is the commandment to keep the seventh day holy as a Sabbath to the Lord.

In the Bible, the span of a day is measured from sunset to sunset. The biblical Sabbath begins Friday evening just before sunset and concludes just after sunset on Saturday night. Many Christians set aside Sunday as a day of worship, so the literal law of keeping the seventh-day Sabbath is not commonly observed. That makes it a good test case for determining whether or not the Law has been canceled.

An Eternal Covenant

In the beginning God created the heavens and the earth in six days. On the seventh day God rested. God did not rest because he was tired but because his work of creation was complete.

> Thus the heavens and the earth were finished, and all the host of them. And on the seventh day God finished his work that he had done, and he rested on the seventh day from all his work that he had done. (Genesis 2:1–2)

The rest of the seventh day was a part of the first week of creation, and thus it is a fundamental part of God's created universe. From the very beginning, when Adam was only one day old, God distinguished the seventh day of the week from all other days, permanently infusing it with holiness and blessing. "So God blessed the seventh day and made it holy, because on it God rested from all his work that he had done in creation" (Genesis 2:3).

There is no biblical indication that this blessing at the time of creation has ever been or will ever be revoked. God initiated and blessed the Sabbath in the garden of Eden before the fall of man, and it is a part of the perfect creation that God saw and called "good." Like heaven and earth, it exists independently of any covenant between God and mankind. It makes sense that after the fall, God would seek to restore this gift that he had "made for man"[50] as a part of the plan of redemption.

Generations later, God moved forward in his plan of redemption by taking Israel out of Egypt to be his own people. And so God revealed to them the blessing of the Sabbath day. The Lord did not wait until the Israelites reached Sinai before he showed them the Sabbath. It was shortly after Pharaoh's army drowned in the sea when he provided the children of Israel with manna for food and instructed them to observe the Sabbath.[51]

When the Israelites reached Sinai, God further revealed himself to them and made a covenant with them. He spoke the Ten Commandments, which include the observance of the Sabbath on the seventh day of the week.

> Remember the Sabbath day, to keep it holy. Six days you shall labor, and do all your work, but the seventh day is a Sabbath to the LORD your God. On it you shall not do any work, you, or your son, or your daughter, your male servant, or your female servant, or your livestock, or the sojourner who is within your gates. For in six days the LORD made heaven and earth, the sea, and all that is in them, and rested on the seventh day. Therefore the LORD blessed the Sabbath day and made it holy. (Exodus 20:8–11)[52]

The Preeminence of the Sabbath

The instruction to celebrate the Sabbath day is repeated throughout the Bible. When the Lord's holy days are mentioned, the Sabbath is listed first.[53] God communicates that observing the Sabbath even takes precedence over providing a livelihood for ourselves.[54] The Sabbath commandment is repeated when instructions are given for building the Tabernacle, showing that even this holy task was to be suspended in honor of the Sabbath.[55] It is one of the laws of holiness, and it is spoken in the same breath as reverence for our parents.[56]

> Therefore the people of Israel shall keep the Sabbath, observing the Sabbath throughout their generations, as a covenant forever. It is a sign forever between me and the people of Israel that in six days the LORD

made heaven and earth, and on the seventh day he rested and was refreshed. (Exodus 31:16–17)

In this passage Sabbath celebration is called "forever." The Hebrew word for this is *olam*, a word often also translated "everlasting" or "eternal."[57] The covenant of the Sabbath will never end.

The Testimony of the Sabbath

From this passage we learn that the Sabbath is a sign. The verse itself states that the sign is given because "the LORD made heaven and earth." In other words, Sabbath observance communicates the truth that the Lord God of Israel is the God who created the entire universe. By showing that our God is creator of all, we express the idea that he is not a tribal deity or merely a god of the harvest or the sea. To say that God created all things is to proclaim the fundamental truth of monotheism: Our God is the only true God, and none other is worthy of worship.

If an entire nation would cease from labor, trade, and commerce[58] on the same day every week, the supremacy of Israel's God would clearly be communicated to the surrounding nations. Other nations would be impacted by Israel's ban on trade, and they would be astonished to see the fields empty of workers. Their curiosity piqued, they would ask about the meaning of this practice, and Israel could respond, "It is because our God created the entire universe and everything in it in six days and rested on the seventh day." By declaring that the God of Israel created all things without exception, there is no room for any other gods.

Someday all nations will acknowledge the Lord as the only true God. Every knee will bow to Israel's God, and every tongue will swear allegiance to Him. In that time (the Messianic Era) everyone will keep the Sabbath. "From new moon to new moon, and from Sabbath to Sabbath, all flesh shall come to worship before me, declares the LORD" (Isaiah 66:23).

Can a single ambiguous statement topple the well-established testimony of the rest of Scripture?

The Prophetic Imagery of the Sabbath

It is fitting that the Sabbath will be observed in the Messianic Era, the one-thousand-year period at the end of the age, when Jesus the Messiah will reign on earth as King. The Sabbath itself is given as an illustration of that future time, at the end of six millennia of redemptive history.[59] The weekly Sabbath is a foretaste of this time when the earth will finally receive a Sabbath rest. The Sabbath is indeed a shadow of things that are to come, and the substance is of the Messiah.[60]

Opposition to the Sabbath

Seventh-day Sabbath observance has been opposed by historical Christianity. Some teach that Jesus broke the Sabbath. However, in the Gospels, this accusation is leveled against him only by his detractors. We should not be quick to side with Jesus' opponents. A careful reading of these narratives shows that he did not break the biblical Sabbath commandments at all; he differed from his opponents as to certain details of how it should be kept. The ministry he performed on the Sabbath actually shows how much he honored and cherished the day. Had he broken the Sabbath, he would have been a sinner and could not be the messiah. He would also have been condemned by his very own teachings.[61]

Some suggest that the Sabbath can be observed any day of the week, pointing to Paul's statement to the Romans that "one person regards one day above another, another regards every day alike. Each person must be fully convinced in his own mind" (Romans 14:5). However, the Sabbath is not the subject of this text. Yet neither does Paul indicate that these days are days of the week. It is likely that he is speaking of minor fast days, since food is mentioned in context. Can a single ambiguous statement topple the well-established testimony of the rest of Scripture?

Although there is no indication of this in the Scriptures, a large segment of historical Christianity has taught that the Sabbath day is to be kept by Christians, but that Jesus changed the Sabbath day to Sunday. A primary proof text is Acts 20:7: "On the first day of the week, when we were gathered together to break bread." But the story in Acts 20 probably did not happen on Sunday, rather Saturday night, when the Sabbath ends and the first day of the week begins. (Remember that in the Bible a new day begins at sunset.) It appears that the community of believers was observing the Jewish custom of ending the Sabbath together with a meal and Scripture study. The evening setting explains why there were so many lamps present and why Paul extended his message until midnight. Note also that "to break bread" is a common Hebrew idiom meaning "to share a meal." There is no indication in this text of a Sabbath-specific sacred observance. In fact, the verse does not make any reference to the Sabbath at all.

Some oppose Sabbath observance altogether since the covenant was made only with Israel. After all, the Torah does say that the Sabbath "is a sign forever between me and the people of Israel" (Exodus 31:16–17). However, the Scriptures state that foreigners and even animals[62] are invited to celebrate the Sabbath day. The prophet Isaiah says that foreigners who voluntarily keep the Sabbath and hold fast to God's covenant will be accepted in God's house.[63] In addition, and as a result of the work of the Messiah, Gentiles are granted a share in Israel's heritage,[64] grafted in,[65] and are included in the commonwealth of Israel.[66]

The Sabbath day is to be observed in every generation by all who fear and love God. It is a sign to all mankind that our God created all things, redeemed us, and is supreme over all.

The Sabbath Is an Eternal Covenant

Therefore the people of Israel shall keep the Sabbath, observing the Sabbath throughout their generations, as a covenant forever. (Exodus 31:16)

Though no longer observed by mainstream Christianity, the seventh-day Sabbath is an ongoing institution that has not been canceled. God permanently infused the Sabbath with holiness and blessing at the time of creation. Observing the Sabbath testifies to the world that the God of Israel is the creator. The Sabbath provides a prophetic picture of redemption. God made the Sabbath a sign of the eternal covenant between himself and his people Israel. Something eternal cannot be abolished. If the Sabbath is still valid and ongoing, then the idea that the Law was canceled when Christ came must be incorrect.

The Law Will Be the Rule of the Messianic Kingdom

Key Points

- By observing the biblical calendar, we learn about the Messiah and God's plan of redemption.
- When the Messiah returns, Israel and the nations will keep God's Law.
- Believers in the Messiah can accept God's kingship and Law even today.

Torah and the Messianic Kingdom

The Torah presents a prophetic picture of the messianic kingdom in two different ways. First, the special days and appointments of the biblical calendar, which are included in the Torah, teach us about God's plan for the ultimate redemption. Second, the Scriptures indicate that when Jesus returns at the end of the age, the Law will be taught, learned, observed, and enforced throughout the world.

The biblical holy days are commandments revealed in God's Law. A lifestyle that is based on the commandments in Scripture is a life of ethics, purity, holiness, righteousness, and devotion in all aspects of human behavior and relationship. In fact, most Christians already observe a substantial portion of biblical Law, either intuitively or intentionally.

The biblical calendar is unique because it synchronizes us with God's rhythm and opens our eyes to his plan. Paul wrote about how the commandments of the Law teach us about future events.

> Therefore let no one pass judgment on you in questions of food and drink, or with regard to a festival or a new moon or a Sabbath. These are a shadow of the things to come, but the substance belongs to Christ. (Colossians 2:16–17)

Sadly, many Bible versions translate this passage very loosely in order to minimize the powerful message of this verse, although the English Standard Version cited above translates the original language fairly well. The New American Standard Bible prefers the wording "mere shadow," even though the word "mere" does not appear in the Greek. The New International Version changes the present tense to past tense to indicate that these are "things that were to come," though the source language communicates that there is much still coming. The final phrase, "but the substance belongs to Christ," can be more literally rendered "and the body [is] of the Messiah." [67]

Ironically, this passage is often used as an argument against celebrating the biblical calendar, even though it states these observances teach us about the Messiah. In addition, people use this verse to condemn others who participate in these observances, even though the verse teaches us not to judge others.

God's Prophetic Plan

Each appointment on God's calendar marks an event in the ultimate plan of redemption. We did not witness the redemptive sacrifice of the crucifixion firsthand, yet we are able to experience it each year by memorializing it on Passover. Some people today may not live until the coming judgment, but we are able to internalize it by rehearsing it every autumn on Yom Kippur.

Participating in biblical holy days gives us a chance to experience the full scope of human history each year, and this gives us a more acute awareness of God's plan for worldwide redemption, helping us understand more about who God is and how he operates. In this way, the holy days deepen our relationship with him.

One might suggest that by simply learning about the holidays, but not observing them, we can attain the same level of understanding. However, the multimedia, full-contact experience of living out the holidays provides a more intimate perspective than mere study. Just as in other areas of life, study alone cannot grant a sufficient level of understanding. Whether learning to drive a car, cook a meal, or sew an outfit, we learn by doing. Celebrating God's appointments enables the truths they convey to sink into our hearts, making them much more than an academic exercise.

Not only do the biblical holidays teach us aspects of life in the coming age, they also train us to participate in those realities presently. In today's fallen world we do not readily see the kingship and dominion of God as it will be when the Messiah finally returns to reign. But on Rosh Hashanah, we declare and acknowledge that God is king and we accept his kingdom upon ourselves even now. Today we cannot fully experience the rest and peace that we will find in paradise, yet each Sabbath we receive a foretaste of that rest and peace.

When these biblical appointments are celebrated with a heart of faithfulness and love, they have the potential to propel us into a deeper walk with our Maker. For this reason, it is to our distinct advantage to observe the biblical calendar.

The Law Will Go Forth from Zion

A second way that the Law provides a prophetic picture of the coming kingdom is that the Torah will be observed by all mankind during the Messiah's reign. Several passages give us

The Spirit serves to sanctify our lives and conform them to God's will.

a chronology of events leading up to the ultimate restoration of Israel, the coming of King Messiah, and the establishment of the full-blown messianic era.

1. Ingathering

This pattern first appears in the law of Moses. We learn that the people of Israel will be gathered back to the promised land. (Though the modern state of Israel is miraculous and prophetic, it is only a hint of the ingathering to come.) Deuteronomy 30 explains,

> If your outcasts are in the uttermost parts of heaven, from there the LORD your God will gather you, and from there he will take you. And the LORD your God will bring you into the land that your fathers possessed, that you may possess it. And he will make you more prosperous and numerous than your fathers. (Deuteronomy 30:4–5)

The ingathering is echoed in Ezekiel 36:24: "I will take you from the nations and gather you from all the countries and bring you into your own land."

The same language is employed in the prophecies of Jeremiah surrounding the New Covenant:

> Behold, I will bring them from the north country and gather them from the farthest parts of the earth, among them the blind and the lame, the pregnant woman and she who is in labor, together; a great company, they shall return here … Hear the word

of the LORD, O nations, and declare it in the coast-
lands far away; say, "He who scattered Israel will
gather him, and will keep him as a shepherd keeps
his flock." (Jeremiah 31:8, 10)

2. Observance of the Law

After this ingathering, Ezekiel teaches that the Messiah will
be king. He also teaches that the people of Israel will obey the
Torah: "My servant David shall be king over them, and they
shall all have one shepherd. They shall walk in my rules and
be careful to obey my statutes" (Ezekiel 37:24).

Indeed, these passages indicate that God will transform his
people by his Spirit and will enable them to walk fully in the
ways of the Torah:

> And the LORD your God will circumcise your heart
> and the heart of your offspring, so that you will love
> the LORD your God with all your heart and with all
> your soul, that you may live … And you shall again
> obey the voice of the LORD and keep all his com-
> mandments that I command you today. (Deuter-
> onomy 30:6, 8)

> And I will give you a new heart, and a new spirit I
> will put within you. And I will remove the heart of
> stone from your flesh and give you a heart of flesh.
> And I will put my Spirit within you, and cause you to
> walk in my statutes and be careful to obey my rules.
> (Ezekiel 36:26–27)

> But this is the covenant that I will make with the
> house of Israel after those days, declares the LORD: I
> will put my law [Torah] within them, and I will write
> it on their hearts. And I will be their God, and they
> shall be my people. (Jeremiah 31:33)

From these verses we see that Israel will be ruled by Messiah and will walk in the Torah by the power of God's Spirit in the coming age. Yet we learn from other passages that it will not only be Israel observing the Torah, but the nations as well:

> It shall come to pass in the latter days that the mountain of the house of the LORD shall be established as the highest of the mountains, and shall be lifted up above the hills; and all the nations shall flow to it, and many peoples shall come, and say: "Come, let us go up to the mountain of the LORD, to the house of the God of Jacob, that he may teach us his ways and that we may walk in his paths." For out of Zion shall go the law [Torah], and the word of the LORD from Jerusalem. (Isaiah 2:2–3)

The prophet Zechariah predicted that in the coming age, the people of the nations will cling to the Jewish people, begging for teaching and direction. The prophet says, "Men from the nations of every tongue shall take hold of the robe of a Jew, saying, 'Let us go with you, for we have heard that God is with you'" (Zechariah 8:23).

Zechariah also declares that all nations will be required to make the pilgrimage for the Feast of Tabernacles (Sukkot) in the messianic era. If they do not, they will receive no rain for that year:

> Then everyone who survives of all the nations that have come against Jerusalem shall go up year after year to worship the King, the LORD of hosts, and to keep the Feast of Booths. And if any of the families of the earth do not go up to Jerusalem to worship the King, the LORD of hosts, there will be no rain on them. And if the family of Egypt does not go up and present themselves, then on them there shall be no rain; there shall be the plague with which the

LORD afflicts the nations that do not go up to keep the Feast of Booths. (Zechariah 14:16–18)

We Can Begin Today

The Bible reveals that the Torah will be an important part of the restoration of all things. But we don't have to wait until the Messiah returns to rehearse our participation in the messianic era. We have been given a down payment of the Spirit of God in our hearts. Instead of passively having God's Law imposed upon us in the future, why not willingly accept it upon ourselves now, out of loyalty to our King? The Spirit serves to sanctify our lives and conform them to God's will. Step by step, as we walk in the Spirit, our lives will reflect the Torah, and the kingdom of God will be made more visible and tangible on earth.

BOUNDARY STONE

The Law Will Be the Rule of the Messianic Kingdom

For out of Zion shall go forth the law, and the word of the LORD from Jerusalem. (Micah 4:2)

he biblical prophets foresaw the kingdom of heaven on earth in the messianic era when the Messiah will return and rule over the earth. In their prophecies, they depicted both Israel and all the nations learning the Law and conducting themselves according to the Law. They foresaw all mankind keeping the biblical calendar and weekly Sabbaths, living under the rule of the Jewish Messiah. If keeping the Law is our destiny in the messianic era, believers in the Messiah can prepare themselves for his kingdom by accepting God's kingship and Law even today.

Boundary Stones

Imagine you are a farmer living in Israel in biblical times. While working in your terraced fields one day, you suddenly stumble over an ancient boundary stone. Why haven't you ever noticed it before? It is partially obscured by the tangled branches of a spreading hedge of thistles, but as you clear back the foliage, there can be no doubt. This upright stone was intended to show where your field ended and your neighbor's began.

Slowly it occurs to you that for the last three generations your family has been cultivating and harvesting a piece of land that is supposed to belong to another family. Now what do you do? Hide the boundary mark and pretend you never saw it? Move the boundary stone over to the edge of the land you have encroached upon? Or do you do the right thing and go to your neighbor and tell him, "I have found an ancient boundary stone set up by our forefathers, and I have come to return to you land that is rightfully yours."

It is rarely easy to do the right thing. You and your father and your grandfather before you have been working that piece of land, clearing it of stones every year, caring for the soil and nurturing a stand of olive trees that are finally large enough to produce well.

But you are a God-fearing man. You remember the proverb that says, "Do not move the ancient landmark that your fathers have set" (Proverbs 22:28). You tell your neighbor. Although you are sad to lose the piece of land, your heart is filled with joy for having done the right thing. "Blessed are those who hear the word of God and keep it!" (Luke 11:28).

The short chapters of this book have uncovered several ancient, theological boundary stones. Some of them we knew about; others we had forgotten.

The Torah
The Law Will Be the Rule of the Messianic Kingdom

Salvation
Salvation Is by Grace

Sin
Sin Is Defined by the Law

The Sabbath
The Sabbath Is an Eternal Covenant

His Servants
God's People are His Servants

The Foundation
The New Testament Cannot Overturn the Old

Not Opposites
Torah and Spirit Are Not Opposites

No Contradiction
Scripture Cannot Contradict the Law

Discipleship
Discipleship Is imitation

Unchanging
God Does Not Change

Like the farmer in the story, we have been operating outside of the boundaries of our faith for a long time. Returning to those biblical boundaries will not be an easy thing to do. Though it may be painful at first, doing the right thing always leads to joy.

There is great joy in studying Torah. When Christians dig into the Torah and begin to understand their faith from the Torah perspective, they are amazed at how the whole Bible suddenly snaps into focus and vivid color. Some say, "I feel like I have a completely new Bible." Others exclaim, "I feel like I've been born again, again!" Still others say, "For the first time, the Bible makes sense to me."

Further Study

The following titles are recommended by First Fruits of Zion for further reading and study:

- *Restoration: Returning the Torah of God to the Disciples of Jesus*
- *Holy Cow! Does God Care about What We Eat?*
- *King of the Jews: Resurrecting the Jewish Jesus*

The following study programs are recommended by First Fruits of Zion for continued discipleship:

- *HaYesod: The Foundation*
- *Torah Club Volume One: Unrolling the Scroll*

Visit First Fruits of Zion online for daily blogs, teachings, and other resources, and to request a free *Torah Portions* reading schedule, and a Resources catalog in print.

- www.ffoz.org
- www.torahportions.org

Glossary of Hebrew and Greek Terms

Word	Hebrew or Greek	Meaning	Strong's Number
a-	α-	(prefix) not, against, without, opposite of, contrary to	G1
anomia	ἀνομία	(noun) lawlessness, being without law, iniquity	G458
athesmos	ἄθεσμος	(adjective) against law/custom, unprincipled, lawless	G113
chet	חֵטְא	(noun) a sin, from a root meaning "to miss a mark"	H2399
de	δέ	(conjunction) but, and, also, even, rather; often omitted in translation	G1161
ehyeh asher ehyeh	אֶהְיֶה אֲשֶׁר אֶהְיֶה	(phrase) "I am who I am," or "I will be who I will be"	H1961, H834, H1961
eved	עֶבֶד	(noun) slave, servant	H5650
Ketuvim	כְּתוּבִים	(plural noun) writings; one of the divisions of the Hebrew Scriptures	Derived from H3789

Word	Hebrew or Greek	Meaning	Strong's Number
mekayem	מְקַיֵּם	(verb) fulfill, establish, perpetuate, uphold; idiomatically, to study and observe (the Torah)	H6965
mevattel	מְבַטֵּל	(verb) nullify, make void, cancel. Idiomatically, to neglect or disregard (the Torah)	H988
Nevi'im	נְבִיאִים	(plural noun) prophets; one of the divisions of the Hebrew Scriptures	H5030
nomos	νόμος	(noun) law, rule, principle, something assigned; often refers to the law of Moses or Jewish law, frequently corresponds with the Hebrew term Torah	G3551
olam	עוֹלָם	(noun) eternity, everlastingness, age; often translated in an adjective sense (eternal, everlasting, forever)	H5769
Shavu'ot	שָׁבֻעוֹת	(plural noun) literally "weeks," also the Hebrew name for the Festival of Weeks or Pentecost	H7620
Sukkot	סֻכּוֹת	(plural noun) literally "booths, tabernacles, or huts," also the Hebrew name for the Feast of Tabernacles or Festival of Booths	H5521
temimah	תְּמִימָה	(adjective) perfect, whole, lacking nothing	H8549

Word	Hebrew or Greek	Meaning	Strong's Number
Tanach	תַּנַ״ךְ	(noun) an acronym for *Torah* ("Law"), *Nevi'im* ("Prophets"), and *Ketuvim* ("Writings"); a term for the Hebrew Scriptures or Old Testament	
Torah	תּוֹרָה	(noun) teaching, guidance, instruction; often refers to the five books of Moses; commonly translated "law"; also frequently corresponds with the Greek term *nomos*	H8451
yarah	יָרָה	(verb) to shoot (as an arrow)	H3384

Endnotes

1 Matthew 7:12, 22:39.

2 Romans 3:23.

3 Romans 6:23.

4 See Matthew 1:21; John 1:29, 3:17; 1 John 3:5.

5 Ephesians 2:8–10.

6 The Septuagint (LXX) uses the term *nomos* to translate *Torah* almost two hundred times.

7 Although it is also possible to define *nomos* as general cultural norms or civil law, both the cultural norms and the civil law of biblical culture were largely based on the law of Moses.

8 The reason I say "applicable" is because there are some commandments that simply did not apply to Jesus; laws concerning menstruation, for example.

9 Romans 8:2.

10 1 John 1:9.

11 2 Corinthians 5:21.

12 Numbers 11:17.

13 Numbers 27:18; Deuteronomy 34:9.

14 Proverbs 3:3, 7:3. Conversely, Jeremiah 17:1 declares that the sin of Judah is "engraved on the tablet of their heart," meaning that the people are so engrossed in sin that it has become a part of their nature.

15 See Leviticus 23:15–21; Deuteronomy 16:9–11, 16 for more information about this festival.

16 Leviticus 19:18; Deuteronomy 6:5.

17 Deuteronomy 13.

18 Galatians 6:13.

19 Also cf. Galatians 6:15.

[20] If Jesus had broken the commandments or even advocated breaking the commandments, the court of law that tried him would not have had to rely on false witnesses to formulate testimony against him.

[21] It is worth noting that when Jesus used the terms "to abolish" and "to fulfill," he was employing standard first-century terms. The phrase "fulfill the Torah" (*mekayem et hatorah,* מְקַיֵּם אֶת הַתּוֹרָה) is best understood as "to study and observe the Torah." Likewise, the phrase "abolish the Torah" (*mevattel et hatorah,* מְבַטֵּל אֶת הַתּוֹרָה) is best understood to mean "to neglect and disregard the Torah."

[22] See Deuteronomy 18:15, 18.

[23] Also see Jeremiah 33:15–18; Isaiah 2:2–3, 11:1–5.

[24] Matthew 5:19.

[25] Gnosticism was an early Christian heresy that taught that the physical world was the creation of a corrupt demi-god (the God of the Bible) and that the true God was utterly unknowable except through the attainment of secret knowledge whereby the immortal soul could escape the fleshly prison of physical matter. In Gnostic versions of Christianity, Jesus is depicted as an agent of the unknowable God, bringing the secret knowledge to earth in order to liberate human souls from the clutches of physical matter and from the God of the Old Testament.

[26] "The LORD" is the standard way for English Bibles to render the personal name of God, roughly transcribed Y/H/V/H. Further reading on this subject has been published through First Fruits of Zion in a book titled *Hallowed Be Your Name.*

[27] *Ehyeh asher ehyeh,* אֶהְיֶה אֲשֶׁר אֶהְיֶה.

[28] Exodus 4:22.

[29] Deuteronomy 14:1.

[30] Deuteronomy 32:5–6.

[31] For more examples see Isaiah 1, 63; Hosea 11:1; Matthew 6; 1 John 2.

[32] For more examples, see Jeremiah 6:19, 9:13, 34:12–22; Hosea 4:6.

[33] Justin Martyr, *Dialogue with Trypho,* chapters 19–23.

[34] For example, see Isaiah 5:24, 42:24; Jeremiah 6:19.

[35] Isaiah 2:3, 66:23; Ezekiel 36:27, 37:24; Zechariah 14:16.

[36] Psalm 19:7.

[37] Psalm 19:9.

[38] Psalm 1:2, 119:174.

[39] Psalm 37:31, 40:8.

[40] Psalm 1:1, 119:1; Proverbs 29:18.

41 Psalm 119:142; Proverbs 28:4.

42 Psalm 19:7.

43 James 2:11–12.

44 Others translate this word "unprincipled" or "wicked."

45 Romans 2:1–2.

46 Romans 2:3–8.

47 Romans 2:9.

48 Romans 2:17–25.

49 An acronym for three Hebrew terms: Law (*Torah*), Prophets (*Nevi'im*), and Writings (*Ketuvim*).

50 Mark 2:27.

51 Exodus 16:23. See also Exodus 16:4–5, 29.

52 Also see Deuteronomy 5:12–15.

53 Leviticus 23:1–3. Also cf. Exodus 23:12, 34:21; Numbers 28:9–10.

54 Exodus 34:21.

55 Exodus 35:2–3.

56 Leviticus 19:3.

57 One might suggest that the meaning of this word is not "eternal" or "forever" but merely "for an age." However, the term is used frequently in contexts that are unmistakably permanent; for example, to describe God's nature (e.g., Genesis 21:33), the duration of his Word (e.g., Psalm 119:89), and the duration of the Messiah's kingship (Isaiah 9:7). Additionally, Jesus and the biblical authors follow traditional Jewish interpretation by dividing the "ages" into two: "this age" and "the age to come" (e.g., Matthew 12:32; Mark 10:30; Ephesians 1:21). They did not see the termination of "this age" as occurring until the Messiah's return.

58 Nehemiah 10:31, 13:15; Jeremiah 17:21–24.

59 Jewish tradition teaches that the world will exist for seven thousand years: the last millennium beginning with the Messiah's coming and ushering in an era of world peace. The book of Hebrews (chapters 3–4) also makes use of the connection between our future rest and the weekly Sabbath.

60 Colossians 2:17.

61 Matthew 5:17–19.

62 Exodus 20:10; Deuteronomy 5:14.

63 Isaiah 56:6.

[64] Ephesians 3:6.

[65] Romans 11:17.

[66] Ephesians 2:11–13.

[67] Most translations emphasize the contrast between these practices and the Messiah by translating the Greek conjunction *de* as "but" or "however." While this is not technically incorrect, we must remember that *de* is a weak adversative, meaning that it does not usually show a sharp contrast. It can even have a continuative sense as in "and" or "moreover." For example, *de* is the conjunction used throughout Matthew's genealogy of Jesus ("and [*de*] Isaac the father of Jacob" in Matthew 1:2). In Colossians 3:13–14, we read, "As the Lord has forgiven you, so you also must forgive. And (*de*) above all these put on love."